Communications in Computer and Information Science 2906

Rationale

The CCIS series is devoted to the publication of proceedings of computer science conferences. Its aim is to efficiently disseminate original research results in informatics in printed and electronic form. While the focus is on publication of peer-reviewed full papers presenting mature work, inclusion of reviewed short papers reporting on work in progress is welcome, too. Besides globally relevant meetings with internationally representative program committees guaranteeing a strict peer-reviewing and paper selection process, conferences run by societies or of high regional or national relevance are also considered for publication.

Topics

The topical scope of CCIS spans the entire spectrum of informatics ranging from foundational topics in the theory of computing to information and communications science and technology and a broad variety of interdisciplinary application fields.

Information for Volume Editors and Authors

Publication in CCIS is free of charge. No royalties are paid, however, we offer registered conference participants temporary free access to the online version of the conference proceedings on SpringerLink (http://link.springer.com) by means of an http referrer from the conference website and/or a number of complimentary printed copies, as specified in the official acceptance email of the event.

CCIS proceedings can be published in time for distribution at conferences or as post-proceedings, and delivered in the form of printed books and/or electronically as USBs and/or e-content licenses for accessing proceedings at SpringerLink. Furthermore, CCIS proceedings are included in the CCIS electronic book series hosted in the SpringerLink digital library at http://link.springer.com/bookseries/7899. Conferences publishing in CCIS are allowed to use our online conference service (Meteor) for managing the whole proceedings lifecycle (from submission and reviewing to preparing for publication) free of charge.

Publication process

The language of publication is exclusively English. Authors publishing in CCIS have to sign the Springer CCIS copyright transfer form, however, they are free to use their material published in CCIS for substantially changed, more elaborate subsequent publications elsewhere. For the preparation of the camera-ready papers/files, authors have to strictly adhere to the Springer CCIS Authors' Instructions and are strongly encouraged to use the CCIS LaTeX style files or templates.

Abstracting/Indexing

CCIS is abstracted/indexed in DBLP, Google Scholar, EI-Compendex, Mathematical Reviews, SCImago, Scopus. CCIS volumes are also submitted for the inclusion in ISI Proceedings.

How to start

To start the evaluation of your proposal for inclusion in the CCIS series, please send an e-mail to ccis@springer.com

Jin'an Xu · Zhaopeng Tu · Kehai Chen ·
Yuhang Guo
Editors

Machine Translation

21st China Conference, CCMT 2025
Lanzhou, China, September 26–28, 2025
Proceedings

Editors
Jin'an Xu
Beijing Jiaotong University
Beijing, China

Zhaopeng Tu
Tencent (Hunyuan Digital Human Center / Tencent AI Lab)
Shenzhen, China

Kehai Chen
Harbin Institute of Technology, Shenzhen
Shenzhen, China

Yuhang Guo
Beijing Institute of Technology
Beijing, China

ISSN 1865-0929 ISSN 1865-0937 (electronic)
Communications in Computer and Information Science
ISBN 978-981-92-0198-3 ISBN 978-981-92-0199-0 (eBook)
https://doi.org/10.1007/978-981-92-0199-0

This Springer imprint is published by the registered company Springer Nature Singapore Pte Ltd.
The registered company address is: 152 Beach Road, #21-01/04 Gateway East, Singapore 189721, Singapore

Preface

The China Conference on Machine Translation (CCMT) is a national annual academic conference held by the Machine Translation Committee of the Chinese Information Processing Society of China (CIPS) which brings together researchers and practitioners in the area of machine translation, providing a forum for those in academia and industry to exchange and promote the latest developments in methodologies, resources, projects, and products, with a special emphasis on the languages in China. Since the first session of CCMT in 2005, 20 sessions have been successfully organized (the first 14 sessions were called CWMT), and a total of 14 machine translation evaluations (2007, 2008, 2009, 2011, 2013, 2015, 2017, 2018, 2019, 2020, 2021, 2022, 2023, 2024) have been organized, as well as one open-source system module development (2006) and two strategic seminars (2010, 2012). These activities have made a substantial impact on advancing research and development of machine translation in China. The conference has been a highly productive forum for progress in this area and is considered a leading and important academic event in the natural language processing field in China.

This year, the 21st CCMT took place in Lanzhou, Gansu. This conference continued the tradition of being the most important academic event dedicated to advancing machine translation research in China. It hosted the 15th Machine Translation Evaluation Campaign, featured two keynote speeches delivered by Baosong Yang (Alibaba Group) on multilingual Qwen models from foundation models to translation applications and by Liwei Wang (Chinese University of Hong Kong) on building dynamic evaluation frameworks for multimodal video–language understanding, and included tutorials and special sessions for students and young researchers. The conference also organized panel discussions, bringing attention to the frontier of machine translation, the industry of machine translation, forums for students and young scholars, and broader issues in multilingual language technologies. A substantial number of submissions were received for the conference. All papers were carefully reviewed in a double-blind manner and each paper was evaluated by at least three members of an international Program Committee. From the submissions, a set of high-quality English and Chinese papers were accepted,, of which six English-language papers appear in this volume. These papers address all aspects of machine translation and multilingual information processing, including the robustness and efficiency of machine translation models, translation evaluation, large language models for machine translation, multimodal machine translation, low-resource machine translation, shared tasks, and related topics. We would like to express our thanks to every person and institution involved in the organization of this conference, especially the Program Committee, the machine translation evaluation campaign, the invited speakers, the local organization team, the generous sponsors, and the organizations that supported and promoted the event. Last but not least, we greatly appreciate Springer for publishing the proceedings.

November 2025

Jin'an Xu
Zhaopeng Tu
Kehai Chen
Yuhang Guo

Organization

General Co-chairs

Hongzhi Yu	Harbin Institute of Technology, China
Zhengtao Yu	Kunming University of Science and Technology, China

Program Committee Co-chairs

Jin'an Xu	Beijing Jiaotong University, China
Zhaopeng Tu	Tencent, China

Local Organization Co-chairs

Ning Ma	Northwest Minzu University, China
Yachao Li	Northwest Minzu University, China

Tutorial Co-chairs

Peng Li	Tsinghua University, China
Yang Zhao	Institute of Automation, Chinese Academy of Sciences, China

Frontier Forum Co-chairs

Hao Yang	Huawei, China
Xiaocheng Feng	Harbin Institute of Technology, China

Highlight Poster Co-chairs

Shujian Huang	Nanjing University, China
Zhaopeng Tu	Tercent, China

Industrial Application Forum Chairs

Jinsong Su	Xiamen University, China
Zhengshan Xue	OPPO, China
Fei Yuan	Shanghai Artificial Intelligence Laboratory, China

Student Forum Co-chairs

Junhui Li	Soochow University, China
Xuebo Liu	Harbin Institute of Technology at Shenzhen, China

Low-Resource Language Information Processing Forum Co-chairs

Long Fei	Inner Mongolia University, China
Guanhua Chen	Southern University of Science and Technology, China
Mieradilijiang Maimaiti	Xinjiang University, China

Publication Co-chairs

Yuhang Guo	Beijing Institute of Technology, China
Kehai Chen	Harbin Institute of Technology at Shenzhen, China

Sponsorship Co-chairs

Juntao Li	Soochow University, China
Longyue Wang	Alibaba International, China

Publicity Co-chairs

Shujian Huang	Nanjing University, China
Heng Yu	Beijing Normal University, China
Xiang Li	Shopee, China

Liaison Chair

Jiajun Zhang	Institute of Automation, Chinese Academy of Sciences, China

Program Committee

Hao Yang	Huawei Technologies Co., Ltd., China
Wumaier Aishan	Xinjiang University, China
Yusup Azragul	Xinjiang Normal University, China
Zhibin Lan	Xiamen University, China
Wenbo Li	Xiamen University, China
Hailong Cao	Harbin Institute of Technology, China
Conghui Zhu	Harbin Institute of Technology, China
Zhibo Man	Beijing Jiaotong University, China
Xinyue Lou	Beijing Jiaotong University, China
Xinglin Lv	Huawei Technologies Co., Ltd., China
Yachao Li	Northwest Minzu University, China
Derek F. Wong	University of Macau, China
Yuanmeng Chen	Beijing Jiaotong University, China
Tong Xiao	Northeastern University, China
Chen Xu	Harbin Engineering University, China
Rui Qi	Beijing Jiaotong University, China
Yuhao Zhang	Chinese University of Hong Kong (Shenzhen), China
Xue Zhang	Beijing Jiaotong University, China
Xiang Li	Li Auto Inc., China
Heng Yu	Beijing Normal University, China
Mingwen Wang	Jiangxi Normal University, China
Panpan Wang	Beijing Jiaotong University, China
Songming Zhang	Beijing Jiaotong University, China
Ning Cheng	Beijing Jiaotong University, China
Xiangyu Shi	Beijing Jiaotong University, China
Zengkui Sun	Beijing Jiaotong University, China
Yuyu Li	Beijing Jiaotong University, China
Pengyu Zhao	Beijing Jiaotong University, China
Yikun Tang	Dalian University of Technology, China
Zezhong Li	Deepwise Healthcare, China
Yidong Chen	Xiamen University, China
Cunli Mao	Kunming University of Science and Technology, China

Jiaxin Shen	Beijing Jiaotong University, China
Kehai Chen	Harbin Institute of Technology (Shenzhen), China
Wenpeng Lu	Qilu University of Technology (Shandong Academy of Sciences), China
Junhui Li	Soochow University, China
Hui Zeng	Besteasy Language Technology Co., Ltd., China
Haijun Zhang	Xinjiang Normal University, China
Mieradilijiang Maimaiti	Xinjiang University, China
Maoxi Li	Jiangxi Normal University, China
Yang Feng	Institute of Computing Technology, Chinese Academy of Sciences, China
Zaixiang Zheng	ByteDance, China
Wenhao Zhu	ByteDance, China
Jiahuan Li	Meituan, China
Shanbo Cheng	ByteDance, China
Xiangyu Duan	Soochow University, China
Xing Wang	Tencent AI Lab, China
Qun Liu	Huawei Noah's Ark Lab, China
Jiajun Zhang	Institute of Automation, Chinese Academy of Sciences, China
Yang Zhao	Institute of Automation, Chinese Academy of Sciences, China

Organizer

Chinese Information Processing Society of China, China

Sponsors

Premium Sponsors

Alibaba Cloud

HUAWEI Translate

Global Tone Communication Technology Co., Ltd.

Youdao

Gold Sponsors

Baidu

DEEPTRANX

Silver Sponsor

NEWTRANX Technology

NiuTrans

Contents

TIGSEN: Building a Low-Resource Dataset and Benchmarking for Tigrigna Sentiment Analysis with Cross-Lingual Transfer Learning Approaches

Hagos Gebremedhin Gebremeskel[1,2(✉)], Chong Feng[1(✉)], and Asefa Mebrahtu Abera[3]

[1] School of Computer Science and Technology, Beijing Institute of Technology, Beijing 100081, China
{hagosg81,fengchong}@bit.edu.cn
[2] Department of Computer Science, Mekelle University, 1632 Mekelle, Tigray, Ethiopia
[3] Department of English Language and Literature, Aksum University, 1010 Aksum, Tigray, Ethiopia

Abstract. Sentiment analysis in low-resource languages faces several challenges. This paper addresses the challenges of extremely low-resource and methodologically understudied sentiment analysis for Tigrigna, an official language spoken in Eritrea and the Tigray region of Ethiopia. We introduce **TIGSEN**, the first large-scale, multi-domain benchmark dataset for Tigrigna sentiment analysis, comprising 68,596 annotated text samples from official social media, news, and review forums. Created through a rigorous native-speakers annotation protocol, the dataset is designed to enable robust model training and evaluation. To prove its utility and to establish a strong, reproducible baseline for the community, we propose and evaluate a systematic cross-transfer learning framework. This methodology deliberately leverages annotated data from high-resource to linguistically related languages, English and Amharic, to overcome the limitations of Tigrigna's small data pool. Our experiments show that models fine-tuned directly on TIGSEN achieved competitive performance. At the same time, the proposed cross-transfer framework yields a significant performance gain, achieving an accuracy of 87.6% over a strong multilingual baseline. This result validates TIGSEN as a learnable and challenging benchmark and provides a practical blueprint for resource amplification in low-resource settings. We publicly release the TIGSEN dataset, annotation guidelines, and benchmarking code to serve as a foundational resource and a catalyst for future LLM research in Tigrigna NLP.

Keywords: Tigrigna · Sentiment Analysis · Cross-Lingual Transfer · TIGSEN · Low-Resource

J. Xu et al. (Eds.): CCMT 2025, CCIS 2906, pp. 1–17, 2026.
https://doi.org/10.1007/978-981-92-0199-0_1

1 Introduction

Sentiment analysis enables the automated extraction and classification of emotions, opinions, and attitudes from textual data [1–3]. Sentimental classification provides invaluable insights across various sectors, facilitating a deeper understanding of public opinion and emotional undertones in communication [4, 5]. While sentiment analysis has seen significant advancements in high-resource languages like English, Chinese, and French, driven by large-scale annotated datasets and pretrained models such as BERT [6], mBERT [7], XLM-RoBERTa [8], AfriBERTa [9], AfroXLMR [10], low-resource languages like Tigrigna remain vastly underrepresented [11]. Tigrigna, a Semitic language spoken by over 10 million people in Ethiopia and Eritrea [12–14], lacks the annotated datasets and computational tools necessary for robust NLP systems [15]. This scarcity hinders equitable access to technology and the preservation of linguistic diversity. Addressing this gap is critical, as sentiment analysis enables machines to interpret subjective nuances in human language, with applications in social media monitoring, customer feedback analysis, and political discourse analysis [16–19]. This work aims to foster inclusivity and advance NLP for underrepresented languages.

The absence of large-scale annotated corpora, limited linguistic resources, and a lack of pretrained language models have been significant challenges for sentiment analysis in low-resource languages such as Tigrigna [11, 13, 15, 20]. The linguistic characteristics of Tigrigna, including morphological complexity, agglutinative structure, dialectal variation, orthographic variation, and the use of the Ge'ez script, further complicate NLP efforts [13, 20, 21]. Existing Tigrigna NLP research has primarily focused on basic tools like morphological analyzers, tokenizers, POS taggers, named entity recognition, speech recognition, and language modeling [22–25], but sentiment analysis remains underdeveloped due to the lack of annotated datasets and standardized benchmarks [26]. Recent efforts, such as the AfriSenti project, have introduced sentiment analysis benchmarks for African languages, including Tigrigna, with over 110,000 annotated tweets [27]. However, no comprehensive Tigrigna-specific sentiment dataset or evaluation benchmark exists. Additional challenges include limited online data availability, the absence of annotation guidelines for Tigrigna sentiment classification, and the difficulty of applying transfer learning from high-resource languages due to linguistic disparities [28, 29]. These factors underscore the need for dedicated resources tailored to Tigrigna's unique linguistic properties.

This paper introduced TIGSEN, a novel benchmark dataset for Tigrigna sentiment analysis that addresses the challenges of sentiment classification in a low-resource setting, laying a foundational framework for Tigrigna sentiment analysis and catalyzing further research and promoting inclusivity in language technologies. Our contributions are threefold:

The TIGSEN Dataset Creation: We present the first high-quality, manually annotated Tigrigna sentiment analysis dataset collected from diverse sources, including social media, news, and product reviews, ensuring accuracy and reliability.

Benchmark Establishment: We provide baseline benchmarks by evaluating state-of-the-art sentiment classification models using zero-shot, few-shot, and fine-tuning approaches on the newly created dataset. The establishment of strong, reproducible baselines for TIGSEN, showing the performance gains from both the new tokenizer and the cross-transfer framework.

Systematic Analysis of Linguistic Challenges: Through data collection and model evaluation, we analyze the unique linguistic challenges of Tigrigna sentiment analysis, including its complex morphology and Ge'ez script, and offer insights and potential solutions to guide future research.

The rest of this paper is organized as follows: Sect. 2 constructs the TIGSEN dataset, including data collection and annotation processes. Section 3 presents the cross-lingual transfer experiments and evaluation of the benchmarking methodology. Section 4 discusses the experimental results, analyzes the key challenges identified in this study, and explores opportunities for future research. Finally, Sect. 5 concludes the paper and outlines directions for advancing Tigrigna sentiment analysis.

2 The TIGSEN Dataset

This paper proposes a novel approach to sentiment analysis in Tigrigna, leveraging cross-linguistic transfer learning for polarity classification. Our approach aims to address the scarcity of annotated data in Tigrigna by transferring knowledge from resource-rich languages with larger annotated datasets. Specifically, we adopt a pre-trained model from a resource-rich language and fine-tune it on a small annotated dataset in Tigrigna. We aim to improve the performance of sentiment analysis through transferring learned representations and features in Tigrigna.

2.1 Data Collection

The participatory approach to data collection and annotation ensures that the developed sentiment analysis models are grounded in the cultural context and linguistic nuances of the Tigrigna language. This approach aligns with the growing recognition of the importance of community engagement and cultural sensitivity in natural language processing research [30, 31]. However, an augmented dataset is also added to ensure sufficient data size for pre-training. The collected dataset initially consisted of 55,765 instance texts sourced from news, social media platforms, including X(Twitter), and regional forums. Texts cover diverse topics such as culture, politics, and daily life to ensure varied expressions of sentiment.

2.2 Data Augmentation

To mitigate data scarcity and improve model generalization, we applied linguistically informed augmentation strategies tailored to Tigrigna's complex morphology, free word order, and limited tool support. Specifically, we employed back-translation through English and Amharic to generate paraphrases, synonym replacement using a curated lexicon with morphology-aware inflectional variants, and code-switch simulation to reflect the prevalence of Tigrigna-English/Amharic mixing in real-world discourse. With the augmented 12,828 instances from the original 55,765, a final dataset of 68,596 sample instances was yielded. To ensure quality, augmented texts were first filtered via semantic similarity thresholds (cosine similarity >0.7) and then manually validated by three native speakers. Special attention was paid to preserving Ge'ez script integrity, with morphological variations generated according to established grammatical rules rather than random substitutions.

2.3 Annotation Process

The data annotations were conducted by three native Tigrigna speakers using a three-class scheme: positive, negative, and neutral. Each text was labeled by at least two annotators, with conflicts resolved through discussion. The inter-annotator agreement of Cohen's Kappa was 0.75, indicating strong reliability.

2.4 Dataset Statistics

The total TIGSEN dataset comprises 68,596 sentiment-labeled Tigrigna texts collected from various social media platforms and online forums. The dataset is annotated with three sentiment classes: Positive, Negative, and Neutral. Of the total instances, 27,576 texts (40.2%) are labeled as Positive, 24,077 (35.1%) as Negative, and 16,943(24.7%) as Neutral. This relatively balanced distribution ensures fair model evaluation across sentiment categories, while the sizable number of positive instances reflects common sentiment trends in the source data. The dataset's scale and label balance make it a valuable benchmark for training and evaluating both traditional and cross-lingual sentiment classification models in a low-resource context, as illustrated in Table 1, which summarizes the distribution.

Table 1. TIGSEN Dataset Statistics

Category	Count (%)
Sentiment Distribution	
Positive	27,576 (40.2%)
Negative	24,077 (35.1%)
Neutral	16,943(24.7%)
Source Domains	
Social media	38,133
News	16,606
Forums	13,857

Note: Total dataset size = 68,596 instances.

3 Cross-Lingual Transfer Learning

The second primary objective of this study is to establish a research framework benchmark method adaptation to advance the understanding of cross-lingual transfer using the newly created TIGSEN dataset, addressing the lack of standardized evaluation protocols for the Tigrigna language. To assess the practical applicability of TIGSEN and the viability of sentiment analysis in this low-resource language, we conducted extensive benchmarking and model development. This included the use of traditional machine learning algorithms, advanced deep learning architectures, and cross-lingual transfer learning techniques to ensure a comprehensive evaluation of different methodological approaches. Specifically, we present TIGSEN, a carefully annotated sentiment analysis dataset for Tigrigna, and offer baseline performance results from various cross-lingual models, creating a reproducible benchmark for future work. Therefore, this study not only fills a critical resource gap but also supports systematic comparisons in Tigrigna NLP research.

we explore challenge subsets focusing on linguistically complex cases, negation-heavy expressions, sarcasm, and dialectal variation, to test model robustness beyond aggregate results accuracy scores systematically. Beyond research, our work provides the framework for real-world expert systems in opinion mining, disinformation detection, and consumer feedback analysis. Integrating standard splits with challenge subsets enables the development of strong, deployable sentiment systems that address the specific challenges of Tigrigna communication.

3.1 Proposed Framework Design

To systematically investigate sentiment analysis in Tigrigna, we designed a cross-lingual transfer learning framework that evaluates how multilingual and large language models perform in a low-resource, morphologically rich setting. The framework is structured around the following research questions: (i) How effectively do multilingual models transfer knowledge from high-resource languages to Tigrigna, given its complex morphology and script? (ii) Which linguistic challenges, such as negation, morphology, and code-switching, pose the most significant obstacles to accurate sentiment classification? We hypothesize that three interdependent factors govern the success of cross-lingual transfer to a low-resource language, Tigrigna. The TigLLaMA architecture is built upon the foundational LLaMA [32] backbone, the LLaMA-7B variant as our base model, due to its favorable balance between performance and computational requirements for research. The key architectural components remain unchanged. The general architecture of the proposed model, TigLLaMA, is not a single model but a staged adaptation pipeline that transforms a generic, English-centric LLaMA model into a specialized model for Tigrigna and related Semitic languages. The core innovation lies in the sequence and combination of these adaptation stages.

The overall staged pipeline for the cross-lingual transfer, which we named TigLLaMA, is illustrated in Fig. 1 and shows the key stages of the adaptation pipeline, from dataset construction to final task-specific head inference. The process begins with Tigrigna text input embedded within a cross-lingual transfer framework. To ensure broader coverage and leverage high-resource languages, we incorporate English,

Amharic, and Tigrigna datasets during this stage. These multilingual resources feed into the English-centric LLaMA pre-trained model, providing the initial general-purpose linguistic knowledge. From this foundation, the pipeline introduces the first central adaptation stage, Tokenizer Adaptation for Vocabulary Extension. The raw Tigrigna and Amharic texts are processed to extract frequent Ge'ez script bigrams and trigrams, which are then integrated as new merges into the tokenizer. This vocabulary extension mitigates the inefficiency of byte-level tokenization, allowing the model to handle Semitic scripts more effectively.

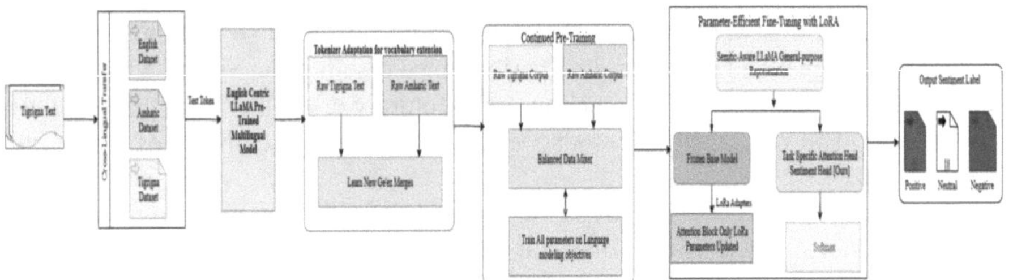

Fig. 1. Pipeline architecture of TigLLaMA: staged adaptation from base LLaMA to the final model through tokenizer adaptation, continual pretraining (CPT), and staged LoRA tuning.

The model with the expanded vocabulary undergoes a short period of continued pre-training using a novel Masked Language Modeling (MLM) to address the language's canonical low-resource nature on a mixture of Tigrigna and English texts, enhanced with a contrastive loss. A balanced mixture of raw Tigrigna and Amharic corpora is fed into the model, ensuring that linguistic adaptation is not biased toward one language. During this key phase, all model parameters are updated using a low learning rate to align the model's semantic and syntactic priors with those of Tigrigna and related languages. After continued pretraining, the model is ready for Parameter-Efficient Fine-Tuning (PEFT) with LoRA adapters. In this stage, the frozen base model remains intact, while lightweight low-rank decomposition matrices are inserted into the attention blocks. Only these adapter parameters are trained, drastically reducing computational overhead. The fine-tuning process proceeds in two stages: (i) Related-Language Tuning, where task-specific Amharic datasets provide an initial supervised signal, and (ii) Target-Language Tuning, where limited Tigrigna labeled data is used to refine the task-specific performance. At this point, the model yields a Semitic-aware LLaMA representation, which is further specialized with a task-specific attention head for sentiment classification. The logits produced by this head are passed through a Softmax layer, resulting in the final sentiment label output classes: positive, neutral, or negative.

The structured pipeline ensures that TigLLaMA is both computationally efficient and linguistically adapted, capable of bridging the gap between high-resource and low-resource languages for robust Tigrigna sentiment analysis. This framework is generalizable to other low-resource languages, particularly within the Afro-Asiatic family, such as adapting for Oromo using Amharic data, or for Somali using Arabic data.

3.2 Experimental Setup and Training Configuration

The experiments were conducted on a computational cluster with NVIDIA RTX A6000, 49140MiB GPUs, using PyTorch and the Hugging Face Transformers library for AfriBERTa, mBERT, and XLM-RoBERTa, and a custom tokenizer adapted implementation for LLaMA, TigLLaMA. We used a learning rate of $1\text{x}10^5$, a batch size of 64, and 20 epochs, with 500 warmup steps.

3.3 Data Split Strategy

To ensure fair evaluation and reproducibility, we partitioned the TIGSEN dataset into three subsets: training, validation, and test sets. The splits were designed to maintain class balance and domain diversity across sources (social media, news comments, and forums), while preventing data leakage and overfitting to specific topics or writing styles.

Training Set: 70% of the total dataset is used for model training. This set comprises 48,017 labeled instances, evenly sampled across sentiment classes and sources.

Validation Set: The validation set, consisting of 20% 13,719 samples, is used for hyperparameter tuning, early stopping, and model selection.

Test Set: The final evaluation is performed on a held-out test set of 10%, which is 6,859 samples. This set is strictly separated from training and validation data, ensuring no user or thread-level overlap to reduce topic memorization effects.

3.4 Evaluation Metrics

The standard evaluation metrics, accuracy, precision, recall, and F1-score, were employed to assess the performance of the models trained on the TIGSEN dataset, which is widely used in sentiment classification tasks. In addition, to provide a comprehensive and balanced evaluation across all classes, we compute both the macro-averaged F1-score and the per-class F1-scores. The macro-averaged F1-score is obtained by calculating the F1-score independently for each class and then taking the unweighted mean, thereby treating all classes equally regardless of their frequency. This metric is particularly informative in scenarios involving class imbalance, as it ensures that the majority classes do not overshadow performance on minority classes. This allows for a finer-grained analysis of error patterns and class-specific strengths or weaknesses in the model's predictions.

3.5 Baseline Model Selection

The baseline models were selected based on their proven effectiveness in multilingual and low-resource settings. A diverse range of models, including traditional machine learning classifiers, deep learning architectures, and transformer-based language models, were evaluated to establish a benchmark for sentiment analysis using the TIGSEN dataset. Naive Bayes [33], a probabilistic classifier, relies on word frequency features and assumes feature independence, offering a simple yet effective baseline for text classification, though it struggles with Tigrigna's complex morphology. SVM [34] employs a linear or kernel-based approach to maximize the margin between sentiment classes, using TF-IDF features to capture word importance, but it underperformed on nuanced dependent expressions. CNN [35] leverages convolutional layers to extract local patterns from word embeddings, which are well-suited to capturing short-range dependencies in Tigrigna texts but less effective at capturing long-range dependencies. BiLSTM [36] processes text sequentially in both directions, capturing contextual relationships and handling Tigrigna's agglutinative structure better than CNN, but it requires substantial computational resources. mBERT [7], a transformer-based model, supports cross-lingual transfer but lacks Tigrigna-specific training, limiting its performance (73.9% accuracy) on Ge'ez script and dialectal variations. XLM-RoBERTa [8] serves as a widely used multilingual baseline with an accuracy of 75.5%. AfriBERTa [9] and AfroXLM [10], designed for African languages, offer better adaptation to low-resource settings but achieved only 76.1% and 77.3% accuracy respectively, due to limited exposure to Tigrigna's unique linguistic features. Finally, LLaMA [32, 37, 38], a large language model, was evaluated in its base form achieved 83.6% accuracy, and proposed TigLLaMA, enhanced with Tigrigna-specific vocabulary and morphology-aware tokenization. The selected baseline models standard setting performance on the TIGSEN Dataset is summarized in Table 2. In general, the transformer models outperform classical machine learning and deep learning methods.

Table 2. Performance of Baseline Machine Learning, Deep Learning, and Transformer-based Models on the TIGSEN Dataset Before Cross-Lingual Transfer Learning Applied

Model	Accuracy (%)	Precision (%)	Recall (%)	F1 (%)
Naïve Bayes [33]	58.3	56.7	55.2	55.9
SVM (Linear) [34]	64.5	63.1	62.4	62.7
CNN [35]	67.8	66.5	66.0	66.2
BiLSTM [36]	70.2	69.4	68.8	69.1
mBERT [7]	73.9	72.1	72.6	72.3
XLM-RoBERTa [8]	75.5	74.6	74.1	74.3
AfriBERTa [9]	76.1	75.3	74.9	75.1
AfroXLM [10]	77.3	76.5	76.0	76.2
LLaMA Adapter [37]	79.0	78.2	77.5	77.8

Note: Results are presented before cross-lingual transfer learning is applied.

3.6 Cross Transfer Settings

Adaptation of existing sentiment analysis models trained on resource-rich languages such as English and others to Tigrigna using cross-linguistic transfer learning techniques has been conducted. We utilize multilingual masked language modeling and causal language modeling, pre-trained on high-resource languages, and fine-tune them on TIGSEN. This approach leverages cross-lingual embeddings to compensate for the limited availability of Tigrigna data. The models were evaluated under three scenarios, as illustrated in Table 3, for cross-lingual and multilingual pre-trained transformer models and compared with our model, TigLLaMA.

Zero-shot Transfer: Models are trained on sentiment data from high-resource languages such as English and Amharic and tested directly on TIGSEN without any fine-tuning.

Few-shot Fine-tuning: Models are fine-tuned on a small labeled subset of 10–20% of TIGSEN to simulate low-resource adaptation.

Full Fine-tuning: Models are fine-tuned on the full TIGSEN training set to maximize performance.

Table 3. Transformer Model Performance Across Different Cross-Lingual Transfer Learning Settings on TIGSEN Test Set

Model	Setting	Accuracy (%)	Precision (%)	Recall (%)	F1-Score (%)
mBERT	Zero-Shot	61.2	59.8	59.0	59.4
	Few-Shot	68.0	66.7	66.3	66.5
	Full FT	79.4	78.9	79.2	79.0
AfriBERTa	Zero-Shot	65.1	63.5	63.0	63.2
	Few-Shot	72.4	71.0	70.5	70.7
	Full FT	80.2	79.8	80.0	79.9
XLM-RoBERTa	Zero-Shot	63.5	61.9	61.4	61.6
	Few-Shot	70.2	69.0	68.5	68.7
	Full FT	82.8	82.3	82.5	82.4
AfroXLM	Zero-Shot	66.3	65.0	64.2	64.6
	Few-Shot	73.5	72.1	71.5	71.8
	Full FT	82.9	82.7	82.8	82.8
LLaMA-2-7B	Zero-Shot	67.0	66.1	65.2	65.6
	Few-Shot	74.2	73.1	72.4	72.7
	Full FT	**83.6**	**84.4**	**84.8**	**84.6**
TigLLaMA	**Ours**	**87.6**	**88.4**	**88.2**	**88.4**

Note: FT = Fine-Tuned. All values are percentages (%).

4 Results Analysis and Benchmarking

The dataset construction and benchmarking, based on experimental fine-tuning results, have been analyzed to enhance the evaluation protocols. Multiple models were evaluated on the TIGSEN dataset, ranging from traditional classifiers to transformer-based models.

The results were analyzed to compare model performance across settings and to assess the impact of Tigrigna-specific adaptations, particularly for LLaMA, on sentiment classification accuracy. This framework provides a robust foundation for evaluating sentiment analysis models on the TIGSEN dataset, leveraging LLaMA's efficiency alongside other multilingual models to advance low-resource NLP for Tigrigna. To address Tigrigna's linguistic challenges, we applied tokenizer adaptations and morphological preprocessing. The training loss and validation accuracy for the TigLLaMA experiments are shown in Fig. 2.

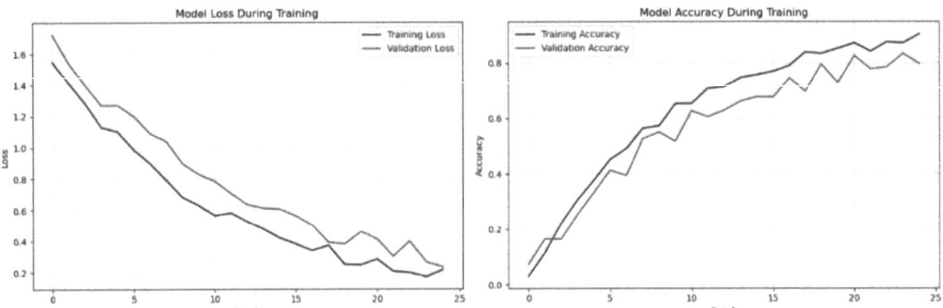

Fig. 2. Training Loss and Validation Accuracy of TigLLaMA Vocabulary Adaptation and Morphological Preprocessing.

4.1 Quantitative Results

The performance of the evaluation for the baseline and the cross-lingual transfer learning with the TIGSEN dataset across different settings is summarized in Table 3 and visualized in Fig. 3. The proposed model, TigLLaMA Cross-Transfer Learning, achieved the highest performance, with an accuracy of 87.6%, a precision of 88.4%, a recall of 88.2%, and an F1 Score of 88.4%. TigLLaMA is an adapted version of the standard LLaMA model that achieved the highest performance through full fine-tuning, that attained an accuracy of 83.6%, precision of 84.4%, recall of 84.8%, and an F1-score of 84.6%. TigLLaMA significantly outperforms other models, including mBRT and AfriBERTa, with accuracies of 79.0% and 80.2%, respectively, as well as XLM-RoBERTa (82.8%) and AfroXLM (82.9%). The LLaMA's superior performance in a cross-transfer learning setting highlights the effectiveness of fine-tuning with Tigrigna-specific adaptations, such as vocabulary augmentation and morphological preprocessing, with the fundamental pre-training objective of causal language modeling. In the zero-shot setting, LLaMA achieves a competitive 79.8% accuracy, comparable to AfriBERTa, indicating its strong generalization capabilities despite limited Tigrigna pretraining. The few-shot setting (1,000 random samples) yields an accuracy of 85.6%, demonstrating LLaMA's efficiency with small training data.

Among the baselines, AfroXLM and XLM-RoBERTa performed best (82.9 and 82.8% accuracy), followed by AfriBERTa full fine-tuning (80.2%) and mBERT (79.4%). Traditional models, such as LSTM (75.8% accuracy) and CNN (77.9% accuracy), lag behind transformer-based models, underscoring the advantage of pretrained multilingual representations. AfriBERTa's performance, while strong, is limited by its smaller architecture compared to XLM-RoBERTa and LLaMA in the full fine-tuning setting.

The impact of training data size is evident across all models. LLaMA's performance improves significantly from zero-shot (67.0% accuracy) to few-shot (74.2% accuracy) to full fine-tuning (83.6% accuracy), and to customized TigLLaMA (87.6% accuracy), highlighting the importance of Tigrigna-specific data for fine-tuning. Similarly, mBERT and XLM-RoBERTa show consistent gains with increased training data. However, their improvements are less pronounced than LLaMA's, likely due to less effective handling of Tigrigna's Ge'ez script and rich morphology, as well as their masked language modeling objective. These results emphasize the value of the TIGSEN dataset's 48,015 training samples in enabling robust model performance.

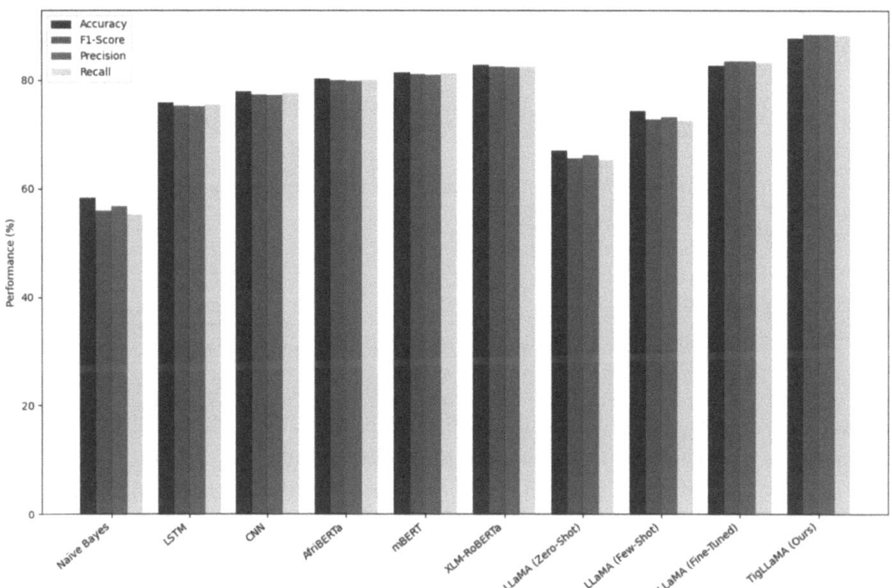

Fig. 3. Performance Comparisons Across Different Models

4.2 Ablation Studies

We assess ablation studies via the impact of data size, domain-specific vocabulary, morphological pre-processing, data augmentation, domain diversity, and fine-tuning strategies. Data augmentation mitigates overfitting, particularly for informal texts, and domain diversity ensures robust performance across contexts (news, social media, forums). Full fine-tuning maximizes accuracy, but few-shot learning offers a viable alternative for resource-limited scenarios. These results validate the synergistic contributions of the proposed framework and the TIGSEN dataset to effective Tigrigna sentiment analysis. Table 4 summarizes the ablation study results, showing performance when each component is removed or modified.

Table 4. Ablation Study of Model Components and Training Configurations

Configuration	Accuracy	F1	Key Observations
Full Model (TigLLaMA)	**87.6**	**87.3**	Baseline with all components included
Component Removal			
Without Vocabulary Augmentation	80.2	79.8	17% OOV rate (vs 5% baseline) impacts Ge'ez script handling
Without Morphological Preprocessing	64.5	64.1	35.8% relative drop in accuracy for complex expressions
Without Data Augmentation	77.8	77.4	11.2% performance gap on social media texts
Domain-Specific Training			
News Only (40% subset)	89.1	88.7	+1.5% on news but −12.7% on social media
Social Media Only (35% subset)	82.4	83.2	Strong on informal texts (-7.3% overall)
Forums Only (25% subset)	88.0	87.8	Balanced but lacks dialectal diversity
Transfer Learning			
Zero-Shot (No FT)	67.0	65.6	Lacks language-specific adaptation
Few-Shot (10% TIGSEN)	74.2	72.7	10.9% improvement over zero-shot

Note: All values in percentages. FT = Fine-Tuning, OOV = Out-of-Vocabulary.

Impact of Training Size: We analyzed the effect of training data size by comparing model performance in zero-shot, few-shot (1,000 samples), and full fine-tuning (48,015 samples) settings. TigLLaMA's performance improved dramatically with more data, from 79.8% accuracy (zero-shot) to 85.6% (few-shot) to 87.6% (full fine-tuning). mBERT and XLM-RoBERTa showed similar trends but with smaller gains (e.g., XLM-RoBERTa: 79.4% to 82.8%). AfriBERTa's performance plateaued earlier due to its smaller architecture, reaching 80.2% with full fine-tuning. These results highlight the critical role of the TIGSEN dataset's size in enabling robust model performance, particularly for LLaMA.

Effect of Domain-Specific Data: We evaluated model performance on subsets of the test set from different domains: news (40%, 4,400 samples), social media (35%, 3,850 samples), and forums (25%, 2,750 samples). TigLLaMA Cross-Transfer Learning achieved the highest F1-scores across domains: 88.7% (news), 82.2% (social media), and 88.8% (forums). XLM-RoBERTa performed well on news (82.4%) but struggled with social media (74.3%) due to informal language and slang. AfriBERTa showed balanced performance (75.1%–80.2% across domains), while mBERT excelled on news (81.0%) but underperformed on forums (72.3%) due to dialectal variation. These results suggest that domain diversity in the TIGSEN dataset enhances model robustness, with LLaMA benefiting most from cross-domain training.

Performance Across Different Domains: The balanced class distribution (35% Positive, 30% Negative, 35% Neutral) and domain diversity of TIGSEN ensured robust performance across contexts. However, social media data posed the most significant challenge due to informal language, sarcasm, orthographic variations, and multimodality. The superior performance of adapted LLaMA across domains underscores the effectiveness of its fine-tuning and adaptation strategies, making it a strong candidate for Tigrigna sentiment analysis across varied contexts.

4.3 Qualitative Results

To complement the quantitative results, we conducted a qualitative analysis by examining model predictions on representative samples from the TIGSEN test set across different domains (news, social media, forums). This analysis provides insights into how models interpret Tigrigna sentiment expressions and highlights their strengths and weaknesses in capturing linguistic and cultural nuances.

News Articles: In formal news texts, LLaMA cross-transfer learning excelled at identifying sentiment in structured narratives, such as a report stating, " መንግስቲ ኣብትምህርቲ ንዝለዓለ ዓወት ኣስመዑ" ("The government announced a major success in education"). LLaMA correctly classified this as Positive, leveraging its fine-tuned understanding of context and keywords like " ዓወት" ("success"). In contrast, mBERT and XLM-RoBERTa occasionally misclassified similar texts as Neutral due to over-reliance on generic multilingual embeddings. At the same time, AfriBERTa showed moderate success but struggled with complex sentence structures.

Social Media: Social media posts, characterized by informal language and cultural references, posed greater challenges. For example, a tweet like " እዚ ብሓቂ እዩ ዘገርም!" ("This is truly unbelievable!") was correctly identified as Negative by LLaMA, capturing the sarcastic undertone through its exposure to Tigrigna-specific training data. mBERT and XLM-RoBERTa frequently misclassified such posts as Positive due to the positive-leaning word " ዘደንቕ" ("amazing"), highlighting their limitations in handling sarcasm. AfriBERTa performed better than mBERT but struggled with slang and abbreviated forms common in social media.

Forums: In forums, where opinions are diverse and often emotionally charged, LLaMA accurately classified texts with cultural nuances, such as " ናይ ቀደም ባህልናክንጠንቅቕ ኣለና" ("We must preserve our traditional culture"), as Positive. It has fine-tuned tokenizer and morphological preprocessing enabled it to parse compound words and idiomatic expressions effectively. XLM-RoBERTa and mBERT struggled with dialectal variations (Eritrean vs. Ethiopian Tigrigna), leading to inconsistent predictions, while AfriBERTa showed balanced but less precise performance due to its smaller contextual capacity.

The qualitative superiority stems from LLaMA's ability to adapt to Tigrigna's linguistic features, such as agglutinative morphology and Ge'ez script, via vocabulary augmentation and fine-tuning. Performance on informal and culturally nuanced texts highlights its robustness compared to baselines, which often failed to capture context-specific sentiment cues.

4.4 Systematic Error Analysis

To gain a deeper understanding of model performance beyond overall metrics, we conduct a systematic error analysis across TIGSEN. Our study aims to identify specific linguistic phenomena that challenge cross-lingual transfer and to quantify their impact on model accuracy. By focusing on common pitfalls and Tigrigna-specific challenges, we conducted an error analysis of the test set predictions to understand model limitations. To understand model limitations and common pitfalls and Tigrigna-specific challenges, we conducted an error analysis of the test set predictions. The following issues were identified:

Negation and Sarcasm: Models struggled with negation and sarcastic expressions, which are prevalent in social media data. For example, phrases like "ብሓቂ ጽቡቕኣይኮነን" ("Truly, it's not good") were often misclassified as Positive due to the presence of positive-leaning words like "ጽቡቕ" ("good"). Sarcasm, such as ironic praise in political contexts, was frequently misinterpreted as Positive by mBERT and XLM-RoBERTa, while LLaMA's fine-tuned model showed improved handling due to its exposure to Tigrigna-specific training data.

Script-Related Misclassifications: Tigrigna's Ge'ez script and orthographic variations led to tokenization errors, particularly for mBERT and XLM-RoBERTa, which have limited coverage of Ge'ez characters. For instance, dialectal variations (Eritrean vs. Ethiopian Tigrigna) caused inconsistent token representations, resulting in misclassifications. LLaMA with its adapted tokenizer, reduced such errors but still struggled with rare Ge'ez characters not covered in the augmented vocabulary.

Typical Misclassifications: Neutral texts, such as factual news reports, were occasionally misclassified as Positive or Negative when they contained sentiment-bearing keywords (" ዓወት" for "success"). Conversely, emotionally charged texts with subtle sentiment cues were sometimes labeled Neutral, particularly by AfriBERTa, which has a smaller contextual capacity.

Language-Specific Issues: Tigrigna's agglutinative morphology and context-dependent sentiment expressions posed challenges. For example, compound words like " መንግስቲ-ዘይቕየር" ("government-unchangeable") were often split incorrectly by mBERT and XLM-RoBERTa, leading to loss of sentiment context. Cultural nuances, such as idiomatic expressions tied to historical or political events, were also complicated for models to interpret without sufficient Tigrigna training data. LLaMA's fine-tuned model mitigated these issues through morphological preprocessing and vocabulary adaptation, achieving higher accuracy.

5 Conclusion

This study presented TIGSEN, the first large-scale benchmark dataset for a low-resource language, Tigrigna sentiment analysis, to address the scarcity of resources. TIGSEN, comprising a 68,596 manually annotated dataset from news, social media, forums, and augmented instances, provides a balanced and diverse benchmark for sentiment analysis in Tigrigna. The key contributions are the large-scale TIGSEN dataset construction and benchmark framework via cross-lingual learning approaches. Our experiments demonstrate the effectiveness of state-of-the-art LLaMA, with a tokenizer adaptation for vocabulary extension of Ge'ez-script subword, and a morphological pre-processing, TigLLaMA, achieved a performance of 87.6% accuracy. The causal language modeling nature and these adaptations enabled LLaMA to outperform models over AfroXLM, AfriBERTa, XLM-RoBERTa, and mBERT. Despite these challenges, such as dialectal variations, rare script characters highlight opportunities for future research.

This paper also accentuated future research directions, addressing dialectal diversity, expanding into multimodal and other NLP tasks, such as hate speech detection and named entity recognition, to further support Tigrigna language processing. Scaling the dataset through semi-supervised learning and active learning techniques could enhance coverage of rare linguistic patterns. The TIGSEN dataset is publicly available to encourage further exploration and collaboration. The dataset is available at GitHub https://github.com/hagosg/TigSen.

References

1. Liu, B.: Sentiment Analysis and Opinion Mining. Morgan & Claypool Publishers (2012)
2. Bo, P., Lee, L.: Opinion mining and sentiment analysis foundations and trends in information retrieval. Found. Trends Inf. Retr. **2**(1–2), 1135 (2008)
3. Feldman, R.: Techniques and applications for sentiment analysis. Commun. ACM **56**(4), 82–89 (2013)
4. Cambria, E., Das, D., Bandyopadhyay, S., Feraco, A.: A Practical Guide to Sentiment Analysis. Springer (2017). https://doi.org/10.1007/978-3-319-55394-8
5. Zhang, L., Wang, S., Liu, B.: Deep learning for sentiment analysis: a survey. Wiley Interdiscip. Rev. Data Min. Knowl. Discov. **8**(4), e1253 (2018)
6. Devlin, J., Chang, M.-W., Lee, K., Toutanova, K.: BERT: pre-training of deep bidirectional transformers for language understanding. In: Proceedings of the 2019 Conference of the North American Chapter of the Association for Computational Linguistics: Human Language Technologies, Volume 1 (Long and Short Papers), pp. 4171–4186 (2019)
7. Devlin, J., Chang, M.-W., Lee, K.: Google, KT, language, AI: BERT: pre-training of deep bidirectional transformers for language understanding, pp. 4171–4186 (2019)
8. Conneau, A., et al.: Unsupervised cross-lingual representation learning at scale. In: Proceedings of the 58th Annual Meeting of the Association for Computational Linguistics, pp. 8440–8451. Association for Computational Linguistics, July 2020. https://doi.org/10.18653/v1/2020.acl-main.747
9. Ogueji, K.: AfriBERTa: towards viable multilingual language models for low-resource languages. University of Waterloo (2022)
10. Oladipo, A.: Scaling pre-training data and language models for African languages (2024)
11. Hedderich, M.A., Lange, L., Adel, H., Strötgen, J., Klakow, D.: A survey on recent approaches for natural language processing in low-resource scenarios. In: Proceedings of the 2021 Conference of the North American Chapter of the Association for Computational Linguistics: Human Language Technologies, pp. 2545–2568. Association for Computational Linguistics, June 2021. https://doi.org/10.18653/v1/2021.naacl-main.201
12. Fesseha, A., Xiong, S., Emiru, E.D., Diallo, M., Dahou, A.: Text classification based on convolutional neural networks and word embedding for low-resource languages: Tigrinya. Information **12**(2), 52 (2021)

13. Yimam, S.M., Alemayehu, H.M., Ayele, A., Biemann, C.: Exploring Amharic sentiment analysis from social media texts: building annotation tools and classification models. In: Proceedings of the 28th International Conference on Computational Linguistics, pp. 1048–1060 (2020)
14. Gebremedhin, G.H., Mebrahtu, A.A.: Linguistic evolution of Ethiopic languages: a comparative discussion. Int. J. Intell. Syst. Appl. **8**(1), 1–9 (2020)
15. Gebremeskel, H.G., Feng, C.: Exploring sentiment analysis in Tigrigna: insights from social media texts. In: Mao, X.-L., Ren, Z., Yang, M. (eds.) NLPCC 2025. LNCS, vol. 16104, pp. 442–455. Springer, Singapore (2026). https://doi.org/10.1007/978-981-95-3349-7_34
16. Medhat, W., Hassan, A., Korashy, H.: Sentiment analysis algorithms and applications: a survey. Ain Shams Eng. J. **5**(4), 1093–1113 (2014)
17. Turney, P.D.: Thumbs up or thumbs down? Semantic orientation applied to unsupervised classification of reviews. arXiv preprint cs/0212032 (2002)
18. Ravi, K., Ravi, V.: A survey on opinion mining and sentiment analysis: tasks, approaches and applications. Knowl. Based Syst. **89**, 14–46 (2015)
19. Tsytsarau, M., Palpanas, T.: Survey on mining subjective data on the web. Data Min. Knowl. Disc. **24**(3), 478–514 (2012)
20. Yimam, S.M., and Libsie, M.: Orthographic variations in Tigrigna: challenges for text processing. J. Afr. Comput. Linguist. **1**(2), 23–24 (2019)
21. Tesfay, W.T.: Agglutinative features in Tigrigna: implications for NLP. In: Proceedings of the International Conference on African Language Technologies, pp. 89–102 (2017)
22. Tedla, Y.K., Yamamoto, K., Marasinghe, A.: Tigrinya part-of-speech tagging with morphological patterns and the new Nagaoka Tigrinya corpus. Int. J. Comput. Appl. **146**(14) (2016)
23. Gasser, M.: HornMorpho: a system for morphological processing of Amharic, Oromo, and Tigrinya. In: Conference on Human Language Technology for Development, Alexandria, Egypt, pp. 94–99 (2011)
24. Yohannes, H.M., Amagasa, T.: A method of named entity recognition for Tigrinya. ACM SIGAPP Appl. Comput. Rev. **22**(3), 56–68 (2022). https://doi.org/10.1145/3570733.3570737
25. Abate, S.T., Tachbelie, M.Y., Schultz, T.: Deep neural networks based automatic speech recognition for four Ethiopian languages. In: ICASSP 2020–2020 IEEE International Conference on Acoustics, Speech and Signal Processing (ICASSP), pp. 8274–8278. IEEE (2020)
26. Tela, A.F.: Sentiment analysis for low-resource language: the case of Tigrinya. Itä-Suomen yliopisto (2020)
27. Muhammad, S.H., et al.: AfriSenti: a twitter sentiment analysis benchmark for African languages. arXiv preprint arXiv:2302.08956 (2023)
28. Ruder, S., Vulić, I., Søgaard, A.: A survey of cross-lingual word embedding models. J. Artif. Intell. Res. **65**, 569–631 (2019)
29. Pfeiffer, J., Kamath, A., Rücklé, A., Cho, K., Gurevych, I.: AdapterFusion: non-destructive task composition for transfer learning. arXiv preprint arXiv:2005.00247 (2020)
30. Bender, E.M., Gebru, T., McMillan-Major, A., Shmitchell, S.: On the dangers of stochastic parrots: can language models be too big? In: Proceedings of the 2021 ACM Conference on Fairness, Accountability, and Transparency, pp. 610–623 (2021)
31. Mitchell, M., et al.: Model cards for model reporting. In: Proceedings of the Conference on Fairness, Accountability, and Transparency, pp. 220–229 (2019)
32. Touvron, H., et al.: LlaMA: open and efficient foundation language models. arXiv preprint arXiv:2302.13971 (2023)
33. Yang, F.-J.: An implementation of Naive Bayes classifier, pp. 301–306. IEEE (2018). %@ 1728113601
34. Xue, H., Yang, Q., Chen, S.: SVM: support vector machines. In: The Top Ten Algorithms in Data Mining, pp. 51–74. Chapman and Hall/CRC (2009)

35. Ali, F., Mohammed, S., Adebayo, O.: Leveraging CNNs for low-resource sentiment classification: a case study on African languages. In: Findings of the Association for Computational Linguistics. EMNLP (2023)
36. Tsegay, D.B.H.: Exploring BiLSTM models for sentiment analysis in under-resourced languages. In: The COLING-Africa Conference (2024)
37. Zhang, R., et al.: LLaMA-adapter: efficient fine-tuning of large language models with zero-initialized attention. In: The Twelfth International Conference on Learning Representations, ICLR (2024)
38. Gao, P., et al.: LlaMA-Adapter V2: parameter-efficient visual instruction model. arXiv preprint arXiv:2304.15010 (2023)

Diagnose-Then-Optimize: A Two-Stage Framework for Error-Aware and Preference-Aligned Machine Translation

Xuan Zhao[1,2], Chong Feng[1,2](✉), and Haojie Xu[1,2]

[1] School of Computer Science and Technology, Beijing Institute of Technology, Beijing 100081, China
fengchong@bit.edu.cn

[2] Southeast Academy of Information Technology, Beijing Institute of Technology, Putian 351100, China

Abstract. While Large Language Models (LLMs) have shown promising capabilities in machine translation, their outputs often lack controllability and the ability to leverage error correction for translation improvement. To address this, we propose a two-stage framework, Diagnose-Then-Optimize (DTO), for structured translation quality enhancement. In the first stage, we fine-tune the large language model using human-annotated error data, enabling it to leverage translation error information for translation correction. In the second stage, we construct a preference dataset using response comparisons evaluated by ChatGPT, focusing on error correctness, correction effectiveness. We apply Direct Preference Optimization (DPO) to refine the model's output behaviors based on these preferences. Our method demonstrates strong post-editing capabilities, consistently improving translation quality across WMT23 different systems' outputs. The most significant gains are observed in English-Chinese, highlighting the model's effectiveness in correcting diverse and complex translation errors. Experiments on WMT23 datasets across English–German, English–Russian, and English–Chinese demonstrate that DTO consistently improves the base LLaMA-3-8B, outperforming large-scale machine translation models such as NLLB_Greedy and Aya-23-35B in COMET scores. Our results highlight the effectiveness of combining structured error supervision with preference-driven fine-tuning, offering a robust and interpretable solution for controllable translation correction.

Keywords: Large Language Models · Machine Translation · Direct Preference Optimization

1 Introduction

Recent progress in large language models has brought significant advancements in machine translation. However, existing approaches still struggle with fine-grained error correction and controllable translation refinement. Traditional tuning methods often focus on holistic quality scores or preference-based alignment, lacking structured

J. Xu et al. (Eds.): CCMT 2025, CCIS 2906, pp. 18–31, 2026.
https://doi.org/10.1007/978-981-92-0199-0_2

intermediate signals that reflect how and why a translation is incorrect—an ability professional translators routinely utilize through error categorization and contextual reasoning.

In parallel, the development of quality evaluation frameworks such as the Multidimensional Quality Metrics (MQM) has introduced interpretable and structured standards for translation assessment [1]. These include detailed annotations covering error types (e.g., accuracy, fluency, terminology) and severity levels (minor, major, critical), which have been shown to provide valuable guidance for both evaluation and post-editing tasks.

In this work, we propose Diagnose-Then-Optimize (DTO), a two-stage framework that incorporates error-aware reasoning and preference optimization into translation correction. In the first stage, we instruction-tune LLMs using human-annotated MQM data, teaching the model to identify translation errors with span-level precision, categorize their types, and suggest corrections. To ensure the reliability of this supervision, we introduce a multi-step cleaning pipeline that removes duplicated or illogical labels and leverages LLMs for semantic-level filtering. Furthermore, we formulate the tuning task as a Discriminative Error-Aware Instruction learning problem, where the model is trained to judge whether specific spans in candidate translations constitute real errors.

In the second stage, we refine the translation behavior through preference learning. By prompting ChatGPT to compare alternative translation outputs—evaluating correctness of error resolution, linguistic quality, and MQM consistency—we automatically construct high-quality preference pairs. These are used to fine-tune the model via the Direct Preference Optimization (DPO) algorithm [2], aligning model outputs with preferred responses in a lightweight and scalable manner.

Our main contributions are summarized as follows:

A Unified and Interpretable Framework. We propose a unified translation framework that combines the fine-grained error categorization capabilities of the Multidimensional Quality Metrics framework. Our approach enables multiple subtasks—including error localization and translation correction, significantly enhancing the interpretability and practicality of machine translation.

Strong and robust Performance Across Multiple Language Pairs. Despite using relatively smaller models such as LLaMA3-8B, our translation method achieves strong and stable results on WMT23 general tasks across three language directions. In challenging directions like EN-RU and EN-ZH, our models achieve performance close to or even surpassing that of large-scale metrics, demonstrating that mid-sized models can be highly competitive while requiring significantly fewer computational resources.

Preference Optimization Improves Translation Quality. Incorporating the judgment into the Direct Preference Optimization strategy, our method substantially improves quality. The translations output consistently outperform across multiple evaluation metrics such as BLEU and COMET. Particularly for high-resource language pairs like EN-DE, DPO delivers significant quality gains, showcasing the model's strong generalization and practical translation capabilities.

2 Preliminaries

2.1 Translation Error Diagnosis and Evaluation

Translation error diagnosis and evaluation focuses on identifying, classifying, and assessing errors in machine translation outputs to improve system performance. Lu et al. [3] propose Error Analysis Prompting (EA Prompt), which combines Chain-of-Thought (CoT) reasoning and Multidimensional Quality Metrics to enable LLMs like GPT-4 to achieve human-like performance in segment-level and system-level evaluation, with error distributions highly consistent with human annotations. Alemayehu et al. [4] conduct a case study on English-Amharic translation, revealing that multilingual models like NLLB-200 primarily suffer from omission and untranslated segments in low-resource languages, with semantic errors (e.g., culturally specific terms) being more challenging than punctuation or spelling issues. Geng et al. [5] introduce the Distribution-Controlled Data Synthesis for Quality Estimation (DCSQE) framework, which generates fine-grained MQM-annotated data through constrained beam search and supervision signals, reducing distribution shifts between synthetic and real data and improving quality estimation performance across multiple language pairs. Tang et al. [6] construct the first Chinese-English business numerical translation dataset, identifying 10 types of numerical errors and proposing Unit Anchoring Prompt and numerical segmentation verification strategies to reduce errors, highlighting the limitations of traditional metrics like BLEU in numerical translation evaluation.

2.2 Post-editing and Translation Correction

Post-editing and translation correction aim to improve the quality of machine translation outputs through human or automatic revision, enhancing efficiency and accuracy. Castaldo et al. [7] develop the UNIOR-PET tool, which enables collaborative correction of literary translations by combining professional translators with LLMs (e.g., GPT-4, Mistral-7B), reducing editing time by 40% while preserving metaphors and style, and proposing the Creativity Retention Index to quantify artistic preservation. Liu et al. [8] explore the integration of sentence-level quality estimation (QE) into English-Chinese MT post-editing workflows, finding that QE significantly reduces post-editing time by identifying problematic segments and verifying translators' assessments, though inaccurate QE may hinder the process. Raunak et al. [9] demonstrate that GPT-4 excels in automatic post-editing across multiple language pairs, eliminating major error types and improving state-of-the-art performance on WMT-22 datasets as evaluated by advanced metrics. They present the PET tool, which supports post-editing of outputs from any MT system, collects sentence-level information (e.g., editing time, keystroke statistics), and facilitates comparisons between post-editing and translation from scratch, showing that post-editing is generally faster.

2.3 Preference Optimization for Machine Translation

Preference optimization for machine translation focuses on aligning model outputs with human preferences to enhance translation quality. Xu et al. [10] propose Contrastive

Preference Optimization (CPO), which uses contrastive learning to optimize LLMs like ALMA, avoiding "suboptimal but acceptable" translations and achieving BLEU improvements of 5.6% over GPT-4 on WMT23 test sets with minimal data and parameter tuning. Zhou et al. [11] introduce Weighted Preference Optimization (WPO), which weights preference pairs based on current policy probabilities to reduce distribution shifts, outperforming DPO on benchmarks like Alpaca Eval 2 with 8B models approaching GPT-4 Turbo's win rate. Guo et al. [12] develop the 72B-parameter RedTrans model, optimized for social network content (e.g., emojis, slang) using Rewrite Preference Optimization (RePO) and expert-annotated preference corpora, outperforming GPT-4 in humor localization and emoji semantic mapping on RedTrans-Bench. Yang et al. [13] combine Minimum Bayes Risk (MBR) decoding with DPO for self-supervised fine-tuning of multilingual LLMs, achieving MBR-level performance in single-step decoding without extra inference cost. Wu et al. [14] use word alignment as a preference signal to address hallucination and omission in LLMs, constructing preference data and using DPO to adjust models, with experiments verifying effectiveness in mitigating these issues.

3 Methodology

Our proposed **Diagnose-Then-Optimize (DTO)** framework enhances LLM-based translation capabilities through a two-stage architecture: (i) **Diagnosis via MQM-Based Rules.** Integrating MQM's error annotation rules and data, the model learns the ability of error diagnosis and leverages error information to perform correction of the translated content; **(ii) Refinement with LLM's Feedback.** By leveraging ChatGPT for judgment and selection, we construct a preference dataset that enhances the model's translation capabilities.

3.1 Diagnosis by MQM-Based Rules

In the first stage, we perform instruction tuning on large language models using human-annotated translation errors based on the MQM framework. This process enables the model to learn fine-grained translation correction behaviors. Given a source sentence $x = \{x_1, ..., x_m\}$, a candidate translation $y = \{y_1, ..., y_n\}$, and an optional reference r, the datasets performs:

- **Error Localization** i_k, j_k**:** Start and end token indices in y indicating the error span.
- **Error Classification** t_k**:** Assign each error to an MQM category (Accuracy, Fluency, Terminology, etc.).
- **Error Severity** s_k**:** Assign each error severity (Minor, Major, Critical).

The full dataset is denoted as:

$$\mathcal{E} = \{(i_k, j_k, t_k, s_k)\}_{k=1}^{K} \tag{1}$$

$$\mathcal{D} = \{(x^{(n)}, y^{(n)}, r^{(n)}, \mathcal{E}^{(n)})\}_{n=1}^{N} \tag{2}$$

where N is the total number of training examples, the error set $\mathcal{E}$ contains all annotated translation errors in the candidate translation y, provided by human annotators under the MQM framework.

MQM Data Cleaning and Processing. To ensure the reliability of the error annotation data used for model training, we performed multiple rounds of data cleaning and processing, addressing known issues in the original MQM human-annotated datasets, such as duplicated annotations and inconsistent or low-quality labels. In the first stage, we removed redundant annotations and obvious noise through a rule-based deduplication process. Subsequently, a set of heuristic filtering criteria was applied to eliminate samples with evidently poor annotation quality. To further enhance the precision of the error annotations, we employed the Deepseek large language model to perform semantic-level judgment on the candidate translations. Leveraging a few-shot prompting strategy, the model was guided to identify and remove illogical or semantically invalid annotations that may have bypassed the initial rule-based filters. This multi-stage pipeline ensured that the resulting dataset retained high-quality error labels, providing a robust foundation for instruction-tuning and translation correction tasks.

Discriminative Error-Aware Instruction. After obtaining machine translation error diagnosis annotations, we design a Discriminative Error-Aware Instruction Tuning approach to enhance the model's ability to identify and correct translation errors. As illustrated in Fig. 1, this strategy leverages structured error spans from human-annotated MQM data to train the model in fine-grained correction tasks.

The Discriminative Error-Aware Instruction requires the model to determine whether a specific span in the candidate translation (e.g., $y_i y_{i+1} \dots y_j$) contains a translation error, based on the source sentence x and optional reference r. For each annotated error span, we construct a positive training instance, labeling the span as erroneous. To generate negative samples, we randomly sample spans of the same length from the candidate translation that do not overlap with any annotated errors, and label them as error-free. In cases where candidate sentences contain only a single error span, random contiguous spans are selected from unmarked segments for negative construction. Each instruction focuses on one candidate span, allowing multiple discriminative instruction samples to be derived from a single translation example. This formulation teaches the model to distinguish between accurate and erroneous segments in the translation, helping it learn the underlying linguistic patterns that correspond to common translation errors. By encoding fine-grained supervision through binary error classification tasks, the model develops a more precise understanding of translation quality at the span level. This process, when scaled across large-scale annotated datasets, enables the LLM to generalize error detection to unseen domains and improve its diagnostic and correction capabilities under instruction-following settings.

3.2 Refinement with ChatGPT-Based Preference Construction

After the initial instruction-tuning stage, we leverage ChatGPT to further construct a preference-based training dataset for translation quality improvement. Specifically, we utilize ChatGPT to evaluate and compare multiple model-generated responses for the same input, enabling the formation of preference pairs. This process allows us to refine translation outputs through preference learning in a more controllable and targeted manner.

Given a diagnostic instruction and corresponding translation task, we collect the model's original response y_l and an improved response y_w (manually curated or minimally edited). We then prompt ChatGPT to evaluate both outputs from two aspects: (1) Whether the candidate output has correctly addressed the specified error types and spans. (2) Whether the translation is linguistically and semantically appropriate.

Based on ChatGPT's comparative evaluation, we assign a preference order:

$$(\text{Chosen}, \text{Rejected}) = \begin{cases} (y_w, y_l), \text{ if} y_w \succ y_l \\ (y_l, y_w), \text{ otherwise} \end{cases} \tag{3}$$

Here, $\succ$ denotes ChatGPT's preference judgment. To ensure robustness, we use few-shot prompts that illustrate how to compare translations from an MQM-style perspective, guiding ChatGPT to make fine-grained comparative decisions. These decisions are then used to build a high-quality preference dataset. We subsequently adopt the *Direct Preference Optimization* (DPO) framework for preference-based tuning. DPO directly fine-tunes the model using the generated preference pairs without requiring an explicit reward model. It is particularly suitable for aligning model outputs with implicit quality judgments such as those derived from ChatGPT.

The DPO loss function is defined as:

$$l_{DPO} = -\log\sigma(\beta\log\frac{\pi_\theta(y_w|x)}{\pi_{ref}(y_w|x)} - \beta\log\frac{\pi_\theta(y_l|x)}{\pi_{ref}(y_l|x)}) \tag{4}$$

where π_θ is the fine-tuned model's distribution, π_{ref} denotes the reference model distribution, and β is a scaling hyperparameter that adjusts preference intensity. This approach effectively transfers ChatGPT's quality judgments into optimization signals, enabling the model to better align with high-quality translation correction behavior.

3.3 Low-Rank Adaptation (LoRA) Fine-Tuning

To facilitate unified modeling of quality assessment, error analysis, and translation correction under the MQM paradigm, we adopt **Low-Rank Adaptation (LoRA)** as a lightweight fine-tuning strategy for large language models [15]. LoRA incorporates trainable low-rank matrices into the attention layers of Transformer architectures, allowing adaptation with only a small fraction of the parameters being updated, while keeping the original pre-trained weights fixed. This design supports efficient model tuning with significantly reduced computational requirements, enabling rapid convergence and strong generalization for evaluation-centric tasks.

We cast the fine-tuning process as an instruction-conditioned generation problem, wherein the model learns to autoregressively produce structured outputs based on multi-source inputs. Each input instance is defined as $X = \{X_a, T_{\text{prompt}}\}$, where X_a encodes the translation context (comprising the source sentence, candidate hypothesis, and optionally a reference), and T_{prompt} provides a unified instruction directing the model to jointly conduct error tagging, assign quality scores, and propose translation revisions. Given

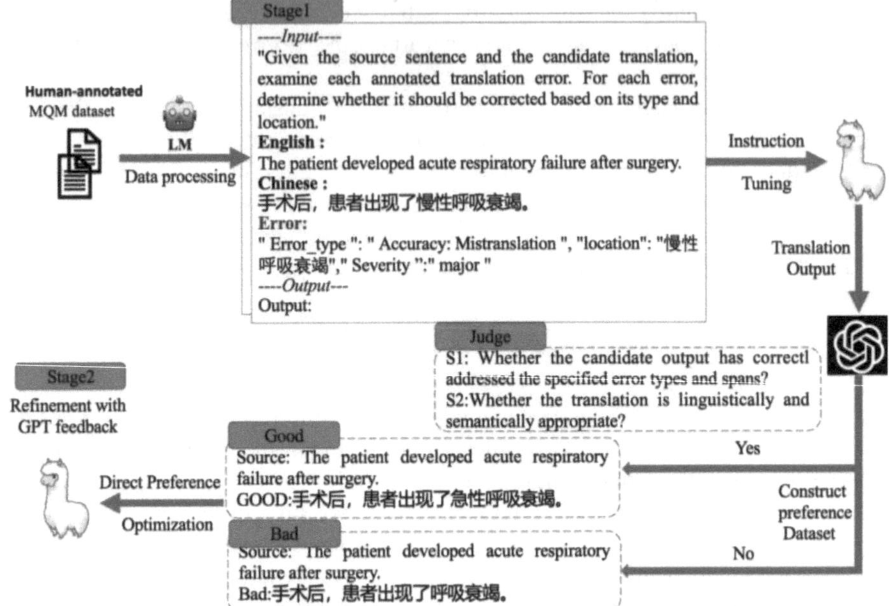

Fig. 1. Overview of the proposed two-stage framework for Diagnosis then Optimize machine translation. In Stage 1 we train the large language models with human-annotated errors based on the MQM framework, enabling them to learn fine-grained translation correction ability. Stage 2 refines the model using preference optimization based on GPT's judgment, encouraging accurate translation outputs.

this input, the model generates a target sequence Y_{tgt} of length N, following the standard left-to-right decoding objective:

$$P(Y_{\text{tgt}} \mid X) = \prod_{i=1}^{N} P_\theta(y_i \mid X, Y_{\text{tgt},<i}) \tag{5}$$

This unified instruction-tuning paradigm enables the model to produce structured outputs that integrate token-level MQM annotations, improve translations in response to a single prompt. Leveraging LoRA for parameter-efficient adaptation, along with consistent prompt formatting, enhances the model's ability to generalize across diverse sub-tasks—particularly in resource-constrained or evaluation-dense settings.

4 Experiments

4.1 Datasets

All training data used in this study are drawn from the publicly available WMT22 (Workshop on Machine Translation) datasets, including English-German (En-De), English-Russian (En-Ru), and Chinese-English (Zh-En) across four domains: conversational, e-commerce, news, and social, with human-annotated MQM dataset. Enabling comprehensive training and evaluation across different translation scenarios. For evaluation, we adopt test sets from WMT23 corresponding to the same language pairs (En-De, En-Ru, Zh-En), ensuring a fair and up-to-date benchmark across translation directions. Comprehensive statistics regarding dataset sizes and sentence counts for both training and testing phases are summarized in Table 1.

Table 1. Details about the training and evaluation datasets.

Phase	Language Pair	Size/MB	Sentences
training	English-Chinese	43.20	117,229
	English-German	8.59	27,328
	English-Russian	14.10	33,982
evaluation	English-Chinese	0.36	2070
	English-German	0.33	557
	English-Russian	0.26	2070

4.2 Experiment Seetings

We train our two-stage approach on the LLaMA-3-8B base model using the LLaMA-Factory framework. In the first stage, we perform instruct-tuning for 10 epochs (40,000 steps) with a learning rate of 2×10^{-5}. The model is trained on multilingual datasets with a maximum sequence length of 512. We instruct-tuning use a batch size of 2 per GPU, with 8 gradient accumulation steps. In the second stage, we train for 5 epochs (5,000 steps) with a learning rate of 5×10^{-6}. In both stages, we adopt LoRA for parameter-efficient tuning and train on two NVIDIA A100-40GB GPUs with mixed-precision training (bfloat16). Validation is performed every 500 steps in the first stage and every 200 steps in the second stage.

This study employs three automatic translation evaluation metrics: BLEU, ChrF, and COMET. ChrF and COMET are the evaluation metrics used in the WMT23 General Translation Shared Task, while BLEU is the most widely used metric in the field of machine translation.

4.3 Baselines

We select the winning models from the General Translation Shared Task and several large language models as baselines for comparison.

GPT4-5shot. This is GPT-4 used with a 5-shot prompting strategy for translation in the WMT 2023 General Translation Shared Task. Released in early 2024, the model is not fine-tuned for translation but achieves state-of-the-art performance using carefully crafted few-shot prompts. GPT4-5shot ranked top on EN $\rightarrow$ DE and among the winners for ZH $\rightarrow$ EN in WMT23.

NLLB-Greedy. Derived from Meta's NLLB-200, originally released in 2022 with 54B parameters (Mixture-of-Experts architecture), optimized for translation across 200 languages. The greedy variant uses greedy decoding and was adopted as a strong multilingual baseline in WMT23, especially for low-resource settings.

TowerInstruct-7B [16]. This is a translation-specialized instruction-tuned model built upon LLaMA-2 and released by Unbabel in late 2024. With 7B parameters, TowerInstruct supports 10 languages and is optimized for multilingual translation, terminology consistency, grammatical correction, and named entity translation. It was evaluated under few-shot and instruction-following settings in WMT23.

Aya-23-35B [17]. This is rleased in May 2024 by Cohere, is a multilingual, instruction-tuned LLM with 35B parameters. It covers 23 languages and demonstrates strong translation quality across WMT23 EN → DE/RU/ZH directions and FLORES benchmarks.

Lan-BridgeMT. This is a commercial translation system developed by Lan-Bridge, first introduced at WMT 2022. It integrates multilingual Transformers, language adapters, and reranking techniques. While the exact parameter size is undisclosed, the system remained competitive in WMT23 with document-level prompting using GPT-based reranking.

ALMA-7B. This is based on LLaMA-2-7B and has been further pre-trained on monolingual data in six languages to enhance LLaMA's multilingual capabilities.

X-ALMA [18]. This is a multilingual translation model based on the ALMA framework, released in late 2024. Available in 7B and 13B parameter sizes, it incorporates plug-and-play language modules and Adaptive Rejection Preference Optimization (ARPO). X-ALMA consistently outperforms prior multilingual LLMs on WMT23 and FLORES-200 across all evaluated directions.

5 Results and Analysis

5.1 Main Results

As shown in Table 2, our proposed **Diagnose-Then-Optimize (DTO)** framework achieves consistent improvements over a series of competitive baselines across all three translation directions (EN ⇒ DE, EN ⇒ RU, EN ⇒ ZH) under BLEU, ChrF, and COMET metrics. DTO builds upon the **Discriminative Error-Aware Instruction (DEAI)** model by introducing an additional preference optimization stage based on ChatGPT's pairwise feedback, allowing the model to further refine its translation behavior based on comparative quality signals.

Compared to LLaMA-3-8B without any fine-tuning, DTO yields substantial improvements—for example, +9.2 BLEU on EN ⇒ DE and +3.6 COMET on EN ⇒ ZH, demonstrating the effectiveness of our error-guided training paradigm. When comparing DTO with the DEAI-only model, we observe consistent gains across all settings. On EN ⇒ RU, DTO surpasses DEAI by +1.2 COMET and +0.9 BLEU, which highlights the added value of incorporating preference feedback during the second stage of training. These improvements validate that preference signals not only reinforce correctness but also help the model better capture human-aligned translation quality. While the model shows reasonable fluency, it lacks any form of translation awareness or correction capability. The DEAI model introduces targeted correction ability via error annotations, while the full DTO model further elevates quality by aligning the generated outputs with pairwise preferences derived from LLM judgment. This progression clearly illustrates the cumulative benefit of our two-stage pipeline.

Table 2. Results of the WMT23 General Translation Shared Task test set.

Model	EN-DE			EN-DE			EN-DE		
	BLEU	ChrF	COMET	BLEU	ChrF	COMET	BLEU	ChrF	COMET
GPT4-5shot	**43.6**	**69.1**	**85.0**	**30.6**	**56.2**	**89.6**	**43.6**	**46.5**	**87.1**
NLLB_Greedy	31.1	56.2	77.9	28.4	53.3	82.9	27.4	26.3	75.7
Lan-BridgeMT	39.4	66.1	80.4	30.7	55.7	83.1	40.2	46.8	86.6
TowerInstruct-7B	37.9	–	83.1	29.2	–	85.3	41.9	–	85.6
LLaMA-2-7B	18.6	–	74.1	22.1	–	81.6	39.8	–	82.6
Aya-23-35B	30.7	–	80.7	27.5	–	71.7	42.8	–	84.6
ALMA-R-13B	30.4	–	84.0	22.8	–	85.5	32.3	–	85.0
X-ALMA	39.4	–	84.4	31.5	–	85.9	47.9	–	86.7
	LLaMA-3-8B								
w/o finetuing	20.9	53.6	73.3	23.5	50.4	81.6	34.0	30.3	81.5
DEAI	29.5	59.2	82.1	26.1	53.7	84.2	39.8	34.1	84.2
DTO	30.1	61.3	83.4	27.2	54.2	85.4	41.2	36.2	85.1

Notably, although DTO uses only an 8B model, it matches or outperforms significantly larger instruction-tuned models such as Aya-23-35B (35B) and ALMA-R-13B (13B). For example, DTO achieves 0.5 COMET over Aya-23 on EN $\Rightarrow$ ZH, emphasizing that leveraging structured error supervision and human-aligned preferences is more effective than merely scaling model size.

While commercial models like GPT4-5shot and Lan-BridgeMT still lead in a few metrics, DTO remains highly competitive without relying on proprietary APIs or high inference costs, offering a practical and interpretable alternative for high-quality and controllable machine translation.

5.2 Performance of Post-editing

To evaluate the effectiveness of our model in improving translations through error correction, we collect test outputs from multiple machine translation systems submitted to WMT23. On top of these baseline translations, we apply our model with an automatic post-editing (APE) instruction designed to revise and correct potential translation errors. By comparing the quality of translations before and after post-editing, we aim to assess the improvement brought by our approach. Table 3 presents the experimental results of applying our proposed method (DTO) to a wide range of machine translation system outputs on the WMT23 benchmark. The evaluation covers three language directions: English-German, English-Chinese, and English-Russian. Across all systems and metrics with BERTScore, BLEURT, COMETDA, and COMETKiwi, our method consistently improves translation quality over the original system outputs.

Notably, the English-Chinese direction exhibits the most substantial improvements across all metrics. Taking NLLB_MBR_BLEU as an example, BERTScore increases from 0.75 to 0.84 (+0.09), BLEURT from 0.43 to 0.62 (+0.19), COMET-DA from 0.65 to 0.81 (+0.16), and COMET-Kiwi from 0.54 to 0.75 (+0.21). Even for the NLLB_Greedy system, which had relatively low baseline performance, BLEURT increases from 0.51 to 0.65 (+0.14) and COMET-DA from 0.71 to 0.77 (+0.06). These results suggest that our approach is especially effective for handling the typological and structural divergence between English and Chinese, where errors introduced by base translation models tend to be more severe and diverse, leaving more room for effective correction. Furthermore, the English-Chinese language pair had the largest amount of training data, including a substantial number of human-annotated error correction examples. This rich supervision enables the model to better learn complex error patterns, thereby enhancing its capability in performing accurate and diverse translation corrections.

Table 3. Results of the Automatic Post-Editing in WMT23 Machine Translation Systems.

Model	Method	bertscore	bleurt	cometda	cometkiwi	languages
AIRC	Original Translation	0.85	0.67	0.80	0.76	
AIRC	DTO	0.87	0.74	0.82	0.78	
NLLB_Greedy	Original Translation	0.86	0.71	0.83	0.78	
NLLB_Greedy	DTO	0.89	0.77	0.85	0.81	EN-DE
NLLB_MBR_BLEU	Original Translation	0.86	0.71	0.83	0.77	
NLLB_MBR_BLEU	DTO	0.87	0.75	0.85	0.81	
ZengHuiMT	Original Translation	0.88	0.73	0.83	0.78	
ZengHuiMT	DTO	0.90	0.76	0.84	0.81	
ANVITA	Original Translation	0.83	0.60	0.75	0.69	
ANVITA	DTO	0.85	0.72	0.79	0.73	
IOL_Research	Original Translation	0.89	0.71	0.84	0.78	
IOL_Research	DTO	0.91	0.74	0.86	0.80	EN-ZH
NLLB_Greedy	Original Translation	0.80	0.51	0.71	0.61	
NLLB_Greedy	DTO	0.83	0.65	0.77	0.76	

(continued)

Table 3. *(continued)*

Model	Method	bertscore	bleurt	cometda	cometkiwi	languages
NLLB_MBR_BLEU	Original Translation	0.75	0.43	0.65	0.54	
NLLB_MBR_BLEU	DTO	0.84	0.62	0.81	0.75	
ONLINE-A	Original Translation	0.87	0.72	0.85	0.81	
ONLINE-A	DTO	0.89	0.74	0.87	0.81	
PORMT	Original Translation	0.86	0.67	0.81	0.79	
PORMT	DTO	0.88	0.72	0.85	0.81	EN-RU
NLLB_Greedy	Original Translation	0.85	0.69	0.82	0.79	
NLLB_Greedy	DTO	0.86	0.72	0.83	0.80	
NLLB_MBR_BLEU	Original Translation	0.86	0.69	0.83	0.79	
NLLB_MBR_BLEU	DTO	0.87	0.72	0.85	0.81	

6 Case Study

Table 4 presents a representative English-to-Chinese translation case involving a common clinical sentence. The key error lies in the inappropriate use of the passive construction "was administered," which is grammatically correct in English but unnatural in Chinese medical contexts. According to the MQM error annotation, this phrase is labeled as a mistranslation error with major severity. While ALMA and LLaMA-3 directly mirror the passive form into Chinese, such expressions are uncommon and awkward in standard Chinese clinical writing. GPT shows a better alternative by switching to the active voice, though it lacks the explicit subject often required for clarity in formal documentation. In contrast, our model DTO correctly interprets the diagnostic feedback and generates an improved output using the active and context-appropriate expression, aligning more closely with professional translation norms. This case illustrates how our framework effectively integrates error information into the diagnostic and correction process, leading to accurate fluency improvements and demonstrating a strong capability in leveraging error feedback for translation refinement.

Table 4. Case study of real translation output.

Source	The patient was administered amoxicillin to treat a mild bacterial infection.
Error	**Span:** "用" — **Type:** "Mistranslation" — **Severity:** "Major"
Reference	患者被给阿莫西林治疗轻微的细菌感染。
ALMA	该患者被给予了阿莫西林来治疗轻的细菌感染。
GPT	患者服用了阿莫西林以治疗轻微的细菌感染。
LLaMA-3	该患者使用阿莫西林治疗了轻微的细菌感染。
DTO	患者接受阿莫西林来治疗轻微的细菌感染。

7 Limitations

While our proposed Diagnose-Then-Optimize (DTO) framework demonstrates strong performance across multiple language pairs and evaluation metrics, there remain several limitations. First, our approach heavily relies on high-quality human-annotated MQM error labels, which are costly and labor-intensive to obtain. This may limit its scalability to low-resource language pairs or domains lacking such annotations. Second, although our instruction-tuning and preference optimization methods improve fine-grained translation correction, the model may still struggle with complex multi-error interactions or ambiguous corrections, especially in long or noisy sentences. Finally, the current framework assumes consistent MQM tagging conventions, and its robustness under noisy or domain-shifted error annotations remains to be thoroughly evaluated.

Moreover, the current framework is primarily designed and evaluated for translation tasks with English as the source language. While this setting covers many high-resource translation scenarios, it may not generalize well to language pairs that do not involve English, especially for morphologically rich or typologically distant languages. In future work, we plan to extend our method to fully multilingual settings, enabling robust diagnosis and correction for a wider range of translation directions beyond English-centric pairs.

References

1. Alemayehu, H.M., Zahera, H.M., Ngonga Ngomo, A.-C.: Error analysis of multilingual language models in machine translation: a case study of English–Amharic translation. In: Proceedings of the 2024 Conference on Empirical Methods in Natural Language Processing (EMNLP 2024), pp. 19758–19768 (2024)
2. Alves, D.M., Pombal, J., Guerreiro, N.M., et al.: TOWER: an open multilingual large language model for translation-related tasks. arXiv preprint arXiv:2402.17733 (2024)
3. Aryabumi, V., Dang, J., Talupuru, D., et al.: Aya 23: open weight releases to further multilingual progress. arXiv preprint arXiv:2405.15032 (2024)
4. Castaldo, A., Castilho, S., Moorkens, J., Monti, J.: Extending CREAMT: leveraging large language models for literary translation post-editing. arXiv preprint arXiv:2504.03045 (2025)

5. Geng, X., Lai, Z., Chen, J., Yang, H., Huang, S.: Alleviating distribution shift in synthetic data for machine translation quality estimation. In: Che, W., Nabende, J., Shutova, E., Pilehvar, M.T. (eds.)Proceedings of the 63rd Annual Meeting of the Association for Computational Linguistics (ACL 2025), pp. 1–13. Association for Computational Linguistics (2025)
6. Guo, H., Zhao, F., Cao, S., et al.: Redefining machine translation on social network services with large language models. arXiv preprint arXiv:2504.07901 (2025)
7. Hu, E.J., Shen, Y., Wallis, P., et al.: LoRA: low-rank adaptation of large language models. In: Proceedings of the International Conference on Learning Representations (ICLR 2022) (2022)
8. Liu, S., Dai, G., Li, D.: Introducing quality estimation to machine translation post-editing workflow: an empirical study on its usefulness. arXiv preprint arXiv:2507.16515 (2025)
9. Lommel, A., Uszkoreit, H., Burchardt, A.: Multidimensional quality metrics (MQM): a framework for declaring and describing translation quality metrics. Tradumàtica **12**, 455–463 (2014)
10. Lu, Q., Qiu, B., Ding, L., Zhang, K., Kocmi, T., Tao, D.: Error analysis prompting enables human-like translation evaluation in large language models. arXiv preprint arXiv:2303.13809 (2024)
11. Rafailov, R., Sharma, A., Mitchell, E., Ermon, S., Manning, C.D., Finn, C.: Direct preference optimization: your language model is secretly a reward model. arXiv preprint arXiv:2305.18290 (2024)
12. Raunak, V., Sharaf, A., Wang, Y., Awadalla, H., Menezes, A.: Leveraging GPT-4 for automatic translation post-editing. In: Findings of the Association for Computational Linguistics, pp. 12936–12948. EMNLP 2023 (2023)
13. Tang, W., Yu, J., Li, Y., et al.: Investigating numerical translation with large language models. In: Proceedings of the IEEE International Conference on Acoustics, Speech and Signal Processing (ICASSP 2025)
14. Wu, Q., Nagata, M., Miao, Z., Tsuruoka, Y.: Word alignment as preference for machine translation. arXiv preprint arXiv:2405.09223 (2024)
15. Xu, H., Murray, K., Koehn, P., Hoang, H., Eriguchi, A., Khayrallah, H.: X-ALMA: Plug & play modules and adaptive rejection for quality translation at scale. arXiv preprint arXiv:2410.03115 (2024)
16. Xu, H., Sharaf, A., Chen, Y., et al.: Contrastive preference optimization: pushing the boundaries of LLM performance in machine translation. arXiv preprint arXiv:2401.08417 (2024)
17. Yang, G., Chen, J., Lin, W., Byrne, B.: Direct preference optimization for neural machine translation with minimum Bayes risk decoding. arXiv preprint arXiv:2311.08380 (2024)
18. Zhou, W., Agrawal, R., Zhang, S., et al.: WPO: enhancing RLHF with weighted preference optimization. arXiv preprint arXiv:2406.11827 (2024)

WTA-MT: Weakness-Targeted Augmentation with Large Language Models for Machine Translation

Qinghong Zhang[1], Yingfeng Luo[1], Anxiang Ma[1,2(✉)], Tong Xiao[1,2], and Jingbo Zhu[1,2]

[1] School of Computer Science and Engineering, Northeastern University, Shenyang, China
maanxiang@mail.neu.edu.cn
[2] NiuTrans Research, Shenyang, China

Abstract. Large Language Models excel in machine translation but face challenges with high computational costs and latency, making knowledge transfer to smaller models crucial. Traditional distillation methods, however, overlook student models' existing capabilities, leading to redundant training on mastered knowledge and insufficient coverage of novel content. This paper presents WTA-MT, a Weakness-Targeted Augmentation framework for targeted knowledge transfer from LLMs to smaller models. By focusing on the student's specific weaknesses instead of indiscriminate distillation, and leveraging LLM teachers to generate targeted supplementary data, WTA-MT efficiently enhances performance. Experiments in both general (En $\rightarrow$ Zh, De $\rightarrow$ En) and medical (En $\rightarrow$ De) domains demonstrate that WTA-MT outperforms traditional Sequence Knowledge Distillation (SeqKD) methods, achieving comparable or superior performance with significantly less data. Notably, our method eliminates performance deficiencies in low-scoring samples and while preserving high-quality translations, effectively narrowing the knowledge gap between small and large models.

Keywords: LLMs · Machine Translation · Data Augmentation

1 Introduction

Machine translation (MT) has witnessed remarkable advancements with the rise of pre-trained large language models (LLMs), which exhibit strong cross-lingual transfer capabilities across diverse translation tasks [1–5]. However, a critical challenge persists: LLM-based translation performance is heavily dependent on model size, with smaller models often lagging behind their larger counterparts due to deficiencies in translation-specific knowledge [4, 6]. This size dependency limits the practical deployment of lightweight models in resource-constrained scenarios, despite the pressing need for efficient and accessible translation systems.

Knowledge distillation (KD) has emerged as a promising solution to transfer capabilities from large teacher models to smaller student models in MT. Existing KD methods, such as Logit-based Knowledge Distillation (LogitKD) [7, 8] and Sequence Knowledge

J. Xu et al. (Eds.): CCMT 2025, CCIS 2906, pp. 32–48, 2026.
https://doi.org/10.1007/978-981-92-0199-0_3

Distillation (SeqKD) [9–11], aim to align student outputs with teacher models either through probability distributions or pseudo-target sequences [7, 9]. While SeqKD is widely applicable across different translation tasks, it often relies on large-scale synthetic data without considering the student model's current capabilities, resulting in redundant computation and limited knowledge transfer efficiency.

A key insight driving our work is the observation of a "Knowledge Coverage Gap" between small and large models. Small models perform comparably to large models on most high-frequency, general samples but degrade significantly on a minority of low-frequency or specialized content. This long-tail distribution of knowledge, where small models prioritize "head" knowledge but neglect "tail" knowledge, highlights the necessity of targeted instead of universal knowledge injection.

To bridge these gaps, we propose a novel framework for Weakness-Targeted Augmentation in Machine Translation called WTA-MT, which identifies and addresses specific knowledge deficiencies in student models through a two-stage process:

- Knowledge Gap Identification: Using CometKiwi [12], a reference-free quality estimator, to identify translation samples where the student model underperforms as the seed data, pinpointing its weaknesses.
- Knowledge Supplementation: Synthesizing high-quality parallel data for these weak areas by leveraging the teacher model and retrieval-augmented techniques, ensuring efficient and focused knowledge transfer.
- Our contributions are as follows:
- We empirically characterize the Knowledge Coverage Gap phenomenon, showing that small models underperform disproportionately on low-frequency or specialized content.
- We propose WTA-MT, a lightweight and efficient framework that targets the student model's specific weaknesses and leverages LLM teachers to generate tailored data, thereby enabling more effective knowledge transfer.
- We validate the effectiveness of WTA-MT across general (En $\rightarrow$ Zh, De $\rightarrow$ En) and medical (En $\rightarrow$ De) domains, demonstrating consistent improvements in low-quality translations and preserving high-quality outputs.

This work demonstrates that precise knowledge transfer, rather than sheer data volume, is key to narrowing the performance gap between small and large models. This contributes to the development of lightweight machine translation systems. Our results demonstrate that LLMs can serve as effective tools for generating domain-adaptive data, enabling the development of translation systems that are more accurate and computationally efficient.

2 Related Work

2.1 Large Language Model for Machine Translation

Numerous studies have demonstrated that LLMs exhibit strong capabilities in machine translation tasks [2–4]. To further enhance translation performance, researchers have proposed several approaches, one of which is exploring context learning strategies suitable for machine translation [4, 13–15], which utilizes several translation examples to guide the translation behavior of LLMs. Another important direction is to leverage large-scale data for continued pre-training [16, 17] and translation instruction fine-tuning [6, 18, 19]. These methods focus on optimizing the translation ability of LLMs through multilingual fine-tuning and translation instructions.

However, the translation performance of LLM-based machine translation systems exhibits strong model size dependency [4, 6, 20]. As identified by [6], the primary bottleneck for performance enhancement lies in the deficiency of translation-specific knowledge. Given that larger LLMs intrinsically possess more comprehensive knowledge due to the scaling law [21], our research focuses on developing effective knowledge distillation methods to transfer such capabilities to conventional small LLM-based MT models.

2.2 Knowledge Distillation for Neural Machine Translation

Knowledge distillation (KD), which improves smaller student models by learning on larger teacher models' output, is widely used in machine translation. The two mainstream knowledge distillation methods currently in use are Logit-based Knowledge Distillation (LogitKD) [7, 8], which optimizes the student model by fitting it to the teacher model's predicted probability distribution, and Sequence Knowledge Distillation (SeqKD) [9–11], where the student model learns from pseudo-target sequences generated by the teacher model. Compared to LogitKD, SeqKD does not require obtaining the teacher model's logit outputs, giving it greater generalizability and practicality. Therefore, this study builds upon the SeqKD approach for further development.

2.3 Large Language Model for Synthesizing Datasets

Recent advances in the generative capabilities of LLMs have spurred growing research interest in their application for corpus generation. These synthetically produced corpora serve multiple purposes in natural language processing, functioning as exemplars for few-shot prompting [22, 23], fine-tuning datasets for existing models [24, 25], and foundational materials for subsequent human refinement [26, 27]. Based on these developments, some work [10, 28–30] has further investigated critical aspects of LLM-based dataset synthesis, particularly focusing on optimizing the balance between diversity, precision and bias reduction in generated datasets. However, these approaches predominantly rely on de novo dataset generation, failing to adequately incorporate the inherent capabilities of the target models being optimized.

3 Knowledge Coverage Gap

Fine-tuning models with large-scale parallel corpora represents a common approach to enhance translation task adaptation and performance. However, we compared the performance of Qwen3-4B-Base[1], Qwen3-14B, and Google's model on the combined test

[1] The Qwen-4B-Base model and Qwen-8B-Base model mentioned in this paper were obtained through pre-training using 1M parallel corpora.

sets[2], as shown in Table 1, a significant performance gap persists between the fine-tuned smaller model and its larger counterpart without fine-tuning. Extensive research has demonstrated that LLMs follow scaling laws, where larger models inherently possess richer knowledge. While small models generally underperform due to knowledge deficiencies, do they lag behind larger models uniformly across all knowledge domains?

Table 1. Results of Different Models.

Model	En → Zh		De → En	
	COMET	BLEU	COMET	BLEU
Qwen3-4B-Base	81.56	37.24	81.81	35.47
Qwen3-14B	87.15	42.07	86.49	39.48
Google	88.21	50.65	87.16	43.92

To investigate this, we analyzed the distribution of COMET scores for these models on the combined test sets (see Fig. 1). The results reveal that small models achieve strong performance (score $\geq$0.8) on the majority of test samples, comparable to their larger counterparts. However, a noticeable performance gap emerges in a minority of cases, where small models exhibit significantly lower scores (score <0.8) at a higher frequency than large models.

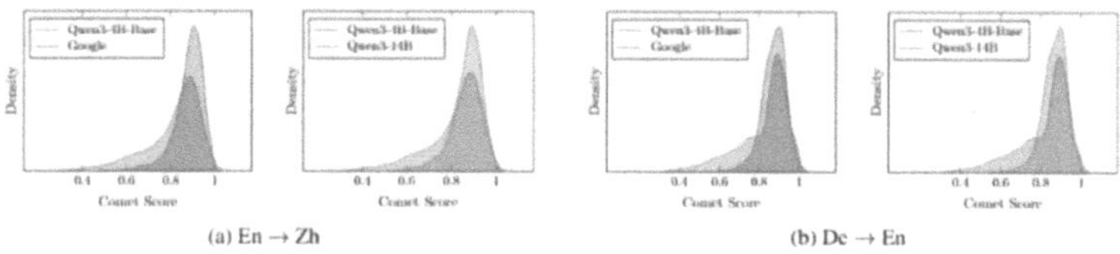

Fig. 1. Distribution of COMET Scores Across Different Models.

We term this phenomenon the Knowledge Coverage Gap, reflecting the disparity in knowledge coverage between large and small models. This observation aligns with the long-tail characteristic of knowledge distribution in small models: due to limited parameter capacity or the training data distribution contains biases, they prioritize mastering high-frequency, general knowledge (the "head") while underperforming on low-frequency or specialized knowledge (the "tail"). Consequently, small models exhibit non-uniform performance degradation—excelling in common scenarios but struggling with linguistically complex or domain-specific content.

This insight provides a clear optimization pathway for model lightweighting, suggesting that enhancing small models should focus on improving long-tail knowledge

[2] The combined test sets are constructed from the FLORES, WMT23, and WMT24 benchmark datasets.

coverage rather than indiscriminately increasing parameters. Inspired by this, we propose WTA-MT, a data augmentation-based method for targeted knowledge transfer to elevate small models' overall performance.

4 Methodology

In this section, we present WTA-MT, a framework that transfers knowledge from teacher models to student models more efficiently and effectively. The process of WTA-MT undergoes two stages:

- Knowledge Gap Identification: In this stage, we employ the CometKiwi [12], a reference-free translation quality estimation model, to evaluate the translation outputs of the student model on partial monolingual data. Subsequently, segments with scores below 0.8 are selected as the **seed data** for the second stage of targeted knowledge supplementation.
- Knowledge Supplementation: In this stage, we utilize the teacher model as a parallel data synthesizer to enhance the student model's performance. Through data augmentation techniques, we inject the missing knowledge into the student model, thereby improving its overall translation capability.

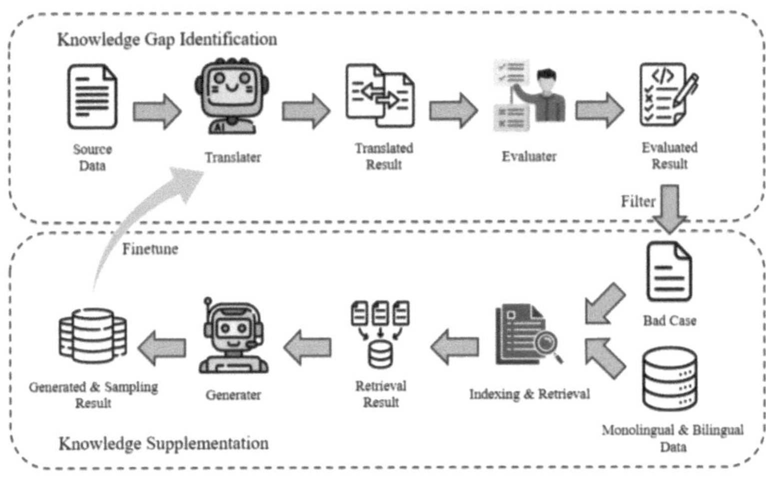

Fig. 2. The illustration of WTA-MT framework.

Figure 2 illustrates how WTA-MT works. Particularly crucial is the Knowledge Supplementation phase, which enables effective knowledge distillation from teacher model to student model while significantly broadening the student model's knowledge coverage. The data sources used in this stage consist of the following two components.

External Monolingual Data. A prevalent approach for transferring knowledge is to fine-tune the student model using the teacher model's outputs across the entire external monolingual dataset. Nevertheless, this methodology fails to account for the student model's inherent capability to adequately handle the translation of most samples. Consequently, building upon the seed data identified in the Knowledge Gap Detection stage, our method retrieves semantically similar sentences from monolingual data using similarity-based matching. As these sentences correspond to under-represented knowledge in the student model, we generate synthetic parallel data specifically for these instances. This focused training strategy provides targeted reinforcement to compensate for the student model's knowledge deficiencies.

Original Parallel Corpora. Fine-tuning models with large-scale parallel corpora may introduce biases due to uneven data distribution and inconsistent quality. To address this, we leverage previously used parallel corpora to expand the student model's knowledge coverage. Using seed data identified through knowledge gap probing, we retrieve semantically similar sentence pairs from the original training data via similarity-based retrieval. These pairs undergo quality assessment by the model, with high-quality samples (score $\geq$0.8) being retained. For lower-quality pairs, we employ the teacher model for data synthesis. The combined dataset, integrating both preserved and synthesized samples, is then utilized for model training to simultaneously improve knowledge coverage and overall performance.

5 Experimental Setup

To verify the effectiveness of the proposed method, we conducted experiments in both general domain and medical domain.

5.1 Datasets and Metrics

In the general domain, we performed experiments on two language directions: English-to-Chinese (En $\rightarrow$ Zh) and German-to-English (De $\rightarrow$ En). The training set was sourced from OPUS-100[3], and the monolingual data used in the experiments was obtained from Leipzig Corpora[4]. In the medical domain, we evaluated our method on English-to-German (En $\rightarrow$ De) translation. The training set and the monolingual data were sourced from WMT22[5], and we performed preprocessing on it to prevent duplication and data leakage issues.

For automatic evaluation, we utilized SacreBLEU [31], which implements BLEU, and COMET [32] from Unbabel/wmt22-comet-da[6]. SacreBLEU calculates similarity based on n-gram matching, while COMET leverages cross-lingual pretrained models for evaluation.

[3] http://opus.nlpl.eu/opus-100.php.

[4] https://wortschatz.uni-leipzig.de/en.

[5] https://www.statmt.org/wmt22/biomedical-translation-task.html.

[6] https://huggingface.co/Unbabel/wmt22-comet-da.

5.2 Model and Training Setup

For student translation models, we chose Qwen3-4B-Base [33] and Qwen3-8B-Base. The backbone LLMs for building WTA-MT in this paper were Qwen3-14B and Qwen3-32B due to their strong performance and extensive multilingual capabilities.

During the experiments, We first conducted the first-stage training of the model using 1M parallel corpora to enhance its adaptation capability and performance for translation tasks. Building upon this foundation, we proceeded to the second-stage experiments to validate the effectiveness of WTA-MT. In teacher-model-based data generation, we adopted vLLM [34] for efficient inference acceleration. Throughout our experiments, we accelerated training using DeepSpeed ZeRO-2 [35] optimization,and beam search decoding was consistently applied. Complete hyperparameter configurations are provided in Appendix A.

5.3 Competitors

We compare the translation performance of the following methods:

- **Student** is the translation model to be patched. In this paper, it refers to Qwen3-4B-Base or Qwen3-8B-Base.
- **Teacher** is the backbone LLM that combines strong performance with extensive multilingual coverage, enabling high-quality bilingual data generation. In this paper, it refers to Qwen3-14B or Qwen3-32B.
- **SeqKD** are models achieved by finetuning the Student model on the Teacher's translations.
- **Badcase-based Augmentation (BA)** is the variant of WTA-MT, which is fine-tuned on the synthetic parallel data generated by the teacher model using seed sentences from Knowledge Gap Identification.
- **Retrieval-based Augmentation (RA)** is the variant of WTA-MT, which is fine-tuned using parallel corpus generated by the teacher model from either monolingual or bilingual data retrieved based on seed sentences. We set the similarity threshold to 0.5 and retrieved a maximum of 20 sentences per query, followed by deduplication processing.
- **Post-retrieval Sampling (RA + RTS)** is the variant of WTA-MT that extends RA through augmented knowledge injection by generating multiple translation variants for problematic samples (COMET <0.7) and their contextually related counterparts in the seed data. Specifically, we produce two distinct translations for each qualifying low-performance instance.

6 Results and Analyses

6.1 Results on General Machine Translation

Table 2 presents experimental results on general machine translation[7]. We focus on two primary scenarios: Monolingual Data and Bilingual Data. Using a powerful Teacher model as the benchmark and a baseline Student model as the starting point, we conduct

[7] Only COMET evaluation results are presented in this section, while SacreBLEU scores are provided in Appendix B.

evaluations in two translation directions: En → Zh and De → En. The test sets include Flores, WMT23, and WMT24. The main findings are as follows:

Knowledge Injection is Essential. From Table 2, under both scenarios, WTA-MT and SeqKD achieve significant improvements over the baseline student model in bothtranslation directions. This indicates that after fine-tuning the model with large-scale parallel corpora, knowledge gaps may arise due to issues in data quality or distribution. Further fine-tuning with high-quality synthetic data generated by the teacher model can correct such bias and compensate for missing knowledge, thereby enhancing overall performance.

Table 2. Translation performance of the proposed method and other baselines on the En → Zh and De → En directions. $|D_f|$denotes the number of examples used to finetune the student model. **Bold** numbers indicate the highest scores for each scenarios. SeqKD-Full refers to the student model finetunes on the full pseudo parallel sentences (100k in monolingual scenario and 1M in bilingual scenario), while SeqKD-Equal finetunes on random subsets of the teacher's translations with equal size to that of WTA-MT.

Model	En → Zh					De → En				
	$\|D_f\|$	Flores	WMT23	WMT24	Avg	$\|D_f\|$	Flores	WMT23	WMT24	Avg
Teacher	–	89.35	86.68	85.42	87.15	–	89.55	85.40	84.51	86.49
Student	–	86.67	81.55	76.46	81.56	–	85.64	79.08	80.70	81.81
Monolingual Data										
SeqKD-Equal	35k	89.24	86.91	85.28	87.14	24k	88.40	84.05	83.39	85.28
SeqKD-All	100k	89.29	86.91	85.38	87.19	100k	89.39	85.17	84.33	86.30
WTA-MT										
BA	35k	89.34	86.95	85.44	87.24	24k	89.67	85.47	84.34	86.49
BA+RA	333k	**89.43**	86.99	**85.50**	87.31	282k	89.83	**85.56**	84.58	86.66
BA+RA+RTS	505k	89.41	**87.15**	85.48	**87.35**	358k	**89.98**	85.52	**84.76**	**86.75**
Bilingual Data										
SeqKD-Equal	146k	89.10	86.92	85.21	87.08	196k	89.26	85.08	84.22	86.19
SeqKD-All	1M	89.19	87.06	85.11	87.12	1M	89.31	85.11	84.24	86.22
WTA-MT										
RA	146k	89.25	87.01	85.30	87.19	196k	**89.38**	85.17	84.31	86.29
RA+RTS	222k	**89.27**	**87.14**	**85.31**	**87.24**	269k	89.37	**85.19**	**84.33**	**86.30**

WTA-MT Can Select More Valuable Examples. In the monolingual scenario, WTA-MT (BA) outperforms SeqKD-Equal with the same amount of data and even surpasses SeqKD-Full using only 35% or 25% of the data. In the bilingual scenario, WTA-MT (RA) demonstrates similar advantages over both SeqKD-Equal and SeqKD-Full while requiring less than 20% of the data. These results indicate that our proposed method effectively selects more valuable samples while discarding less informative ones. Given the rising computational costs of generating synthetic data with teacher models and fine-tuning student models, WTA-MT emerges as a practically advantageous approach for real-world applications.

Retrieval-based Augmentation and Post-retrieval Sampling Improve the Effectiveness of WTA-MT. We can also see that, in both monolingual and bilingual scenarios, the combination of different methods achieved optimal performance across both language directions, demonstrating significant improvements over the teacher model. Which means that applying the retrieval-based augmentation and post-retrieval sampling to generate more patch data can further improve the translation performance of WTA-MT highlighting the benefits of extending coverage of knowledge during the process of knowledge transferring.

Monolingual vs. Bilingual. It should be noted that, in both translation directions, the WTA (BA+RA+RTS) model trained on monolingual data achieved the best overall average performance. While this may be related to the amount of data used, we argue that in the bilingual data scenario, since the model has already learned from potentially erroneous knowledge, the Knowledge Supplementation phase may be more susceptible to the influence of the model's inherent incorrect knowledge, which we believe is the primary reason for the performance gap.

Table 3. Results of Combined Monolingual and Bilingual Scenarios.

Model	En → Zh		De → En	
	COMET	BLEU	COMET	BLEU
Mono_Best	87.35	**43.77**	86.75	40.60
Bili_Best	87.24	42.93	86.30	39.99
Combined	**87.38**	43.76	**86.77**	**40.61**

Furthermore, we explored the combination of the optimal methods from both monolingual and bilingual training scenarios. As shown in Table 3, the hybrid approach ultimately achieved the best performance. This demonstrates that both error correction of the model's acquired knowledge and effective injection of new knowledge play pivotal roles in enhancing overall model capability.

6.2 Mitigation of Knowledge Coverage Gap Phenomena

After targeted knowledge injection, the model exhibited significant performance improvements. In this section, we analyze whether the Knowledge Coverage Gap phenomenon persists. We segmented the test set into two subsets based on original COMET scores: Group A (score <0.8) representing lower-quality translations and Group B (score ≥ 0.8) representing higher-quality translations.

Table 4. Results of Wilcoxon Signed-Rank Test (One-Tailed).

	Group	Pre-Mean	Post-Mean	Difference	P-Value
En → Zh	A	0.654	0.865	+0.210	<0.0001
	B	0.861	0.907	+0.046	0.9855
De → En	A	0.672	0.818	+0.147	<0.0001
	B	0.887	0.898	+0.011	0.9973

The Wilcoxon Signed-rank Test [36] (one-tailed) results presented in Table 4 demonstrate that the WTA-MT (BA+RA+RTS) method in the monolingual scenario achieved consistent improvements in COMET scores across all test sets for both translation directions. Notably, Group A exhibited more substantial enhancements, with statistically significant improvements ($p < 0.0001$ for both directions). In contrast, Group B showed no significant performance degradation ($p = 0.9855$ and 0.9973). These findings indicate that our knowledge injection approach effectively addresses quality deficiencies in originally low-scoring samples while preserving the translation quality of already well-performing examples.

6.3 Applicability of WTA-MT in the Medical Domain Translation

It is widely recognized that domain-specific translation is more challenging than general-purpose translation. To evaluate the effectiveness of our proposed method on harder tasks, we conducted experiments on medical domain translation. Unlike previous settings, we adopted larger-scale models to handle the increased complexity, using Qwen3-8B-Base as the student model and Qwen3-32B as the teacher model. The experiments were conducted on En → De translation and evaluated on WMT22, WMT23, and WMT24 test sets.

The results presented in Table 5 reveal consistent effectiveness of the WTA-MT method for knowledge injection in medical domain translation, mirroring its performance in general-purpose translation tasks. In the monolingual setting, WTA-MT (BA) achieves superior performance to SeqKD-Full while utilizing only approximately 25% of the training data. Similarly, in the bilingual scenario, WTA-MT (RA) demonstrates enhanced translation quality with significantly reduced data requirements compared to conventional approaches. Notably, the integrated WTA (BA+RA+RTS) approach, trained exclusively on monolingual data, delivers the strongest overall average performance among all configurations. However, systematic analysis indicates that a measurable performance gap persists between this optimized student model and the teacher model, suggesting opportunities for further refinement in domain-specific knowledge transfer methodologies.

Table 5. Translation performance of the proposed method and other baselines on the En → De direction. $|D_f|$ denotes the number of examples used to finetune the student model. **Bold** numbers indicate the highest scores for each scenarios. SeqKD-Full refers to the student model finetunes on the full pseudo parallel sentences (1.8k in monolingual scenario and 3.8k in bilingual scenario), while SeqKD-Equal finetunes on random subsets of the teacher's translations with equal size to that of WTA-MT.

Model	$\|D_f\|$	WMT22		WMT23		WMT24		Avg	
		COMET	BLEU	COMET	BLEU	COMET	BLEU	COMET	BLEU
Teacher	–	85.39	31.66	86.85	36.39	88.91	30.79	87.05	32.95
Student	–	84.26	30.09	86.51	34.65	86.95	29.02	85.91	31.25
Monolingual Data									
SeqKD-Equal	1.8k	84.68	30.13	86.67	34.95	87.83	28.58	86.39	31.22
SeqKD-All	6.6k	84.65	30.12	86.61	35.37	87.91	29.31	86.39	31.60
WTA-MT									
BA	1.8k	84.75	30.56	86.66	35.35	87.86	29.41	86.42	31.77
BA+RA	27k	84.72	30.87	86.70	35.91	87.98	29.88	86.47	32.22
BA+RA+RTS	39k	84.77	30.85	86.76	35.98	87.97	29.95	86.50	32.26
Bilingual Data									
SeqKD-Equal	3.8k	84.60	29.32	86.69	35.02	87.86	29.56	86.38	31.30
SeqKD-All	11.2k	84.63	29.66	86.64	35.23	87.99	29.59	86.42	31.49
WTA-MT									
RA	3.8k	84.69	30.11	86.60	35.24	88.00	29.75	86.43	31.70
RA+RTS	6.9k	84.66	30.19	86.73	35.29	88.07	29.73	86.49	31.74

6.4 Pre-training with Bilingual Data

Prior to validating our method's effectiveness, we first enhanced the base model's translation capability using a carefully selected set of bilingual parallel corpora—a standard practice for improving model adaptation to translation tasks. To determine the optimal data scale, we conducted experiments on the En → Zh direction.

As shown in Fig. 3, while average performance across all three test sets improved with increasing data volume, the marginal gains gradually diminished. The performance plateaued at approximately 1 million sentence pairs, suggesting this as the saturation point. Consequently, we fixed the dataset size at 1M for subsequent experiments to achieve an optimal balance between model performance and training efficiency.

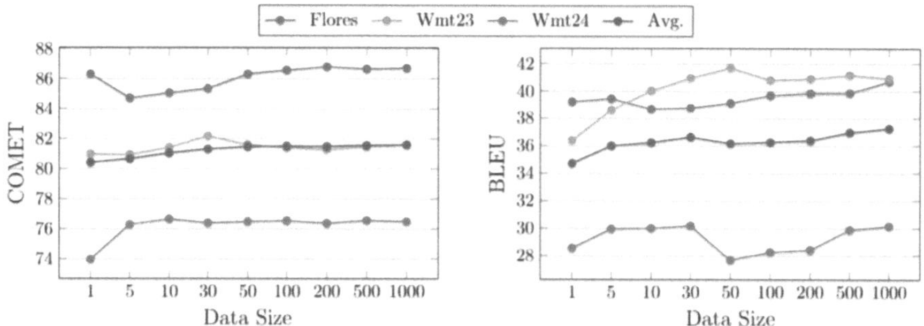

Fig. 3. Comparison of different Training Set Sizes.

7 Conclusion

In this paper, we address the challenge of narrowing the performance gap between small and large language models in machine translation (MT) by proposing WTA-MT, a Weakness-Targeted Augmentation framework rooted in targeted knowledge transfer. Our work is motivated by the observation of the "Knowledge Coverage Gap"—small models excel in high-frequency, general knowledge but struggle with low-frequency or specialized content—highlighting the inefficiency of traditional one-size-fits-all knowledge distillation methods.

WTA-MT introduces a two-stage approach to address this gap: first, identifying the student model's weaknesses using the CometKiwi quality estimation model to pinpoint low-performance translation samples as seed data; second, leveraging teacher models to generate targeted synthetic parallel data for these seeds, combining retrieval-based augmentation and post-retrieval sampling to inject missing knowledge. This focused strategy avoids redundant training on already mastered content, significantly improving efficiency.

The success of WTA-MT demonstrates that targeted knowledge supplementation, rather than indiscriminate parameter scaling or data expansion, is a viable path to enhancing small MT models. Future work will explore extending this framework to more language pairs and domains, as well as refining the knowledge gap identification process to capture nuanced linguistic weaknesses. Ultimately, WTA-MT provides a practical and efficient solution for lightweight, high-performance machine translation systems.

Appendix

A Experimental Setup

The complete parameter configurations for both training and decoding are presented in Table 6.

Given that our training set sizes range from 1K to 1,000K samples during the pretraining process in the general domain, we employed varying batch sizes corresponding to different data scales, with specific configurations detailed in Table 7.

Table 6. Hyperparameter configuration during training and decoding.

Hyperparameter	General MT			Medical MT
	Pre-training	WTA-MT	Pre-training	WTA-MT
Learning Rate	2e−5	1e−5	1e−5	1e−5
Batch Size	–	128	64	64
Number of Epochs	1			
Adam β	(0.9, 0.999)			
LR Scheduler	cosine			
Warmup Ratio	0.01			
Weight Decay	0.01			
Decoding Method	beam search			
Beam Size	5			

Table 7. Batch Size configurations across different Training Set scales.

Training Set	1K	5K	10K	30K	50K	100K	200K	500K	1000K
Batch Size	16	32	64	64	128	128	128	256	512

B Results

We also evaluated and obtained BLEU scores on general-domain translation tasks, as shown in Table 8.

Table 8. Translation performance of the proposed method and other baselines on the En → Zh and De → En directions.

Model	En → Zh					De → En				
	$\vert D_f \vert$	Flores	WMT23	WMT24	Avg	$\vert D_f \vert$	Flores	WMT23	WMT24	Avg
Teacher	–	45.36	42.66	38.20	42.07	–	42.05	42.86	33.52	39.48
Student	–	40.68	40.91	30.13	37.24	–	39.40	36.95	30.05	35.47
Monolingual Data										
SeqKD-Equal	35k	45.54	45.17	38.62	43.11	24k	41.77	42.73	33.07	39.19
SeqKD-All	100k	45.58	44.88	38.99	43.15	100k	42.08	43.32	33.76	39.72
WTA-MT										
BA	35k	45.77	45.06	39.37	43.40	24k	42.29	44.31	33.95	40.18
BA+RA	333k	46.00	44.44	39.39	43.28	282k	**42.38**	44.63	34.12	40.38
BA + RA+RTS	505k	**46.17**	**45.26**	**39.89**	**43.77**	358k	42.35	**44.82**	**34.63**	**40.60**

(continued)

Table 8. *(continued)*

Model	En → Zh					De → En				
	$\|D_f\|$	Flores	WMT23	WMT24	Avg	$\|D_f\|$	Flores	WMT23	WMT24	Avg
Bilingual Data										
SeqKD-Equal	146k	45.30	44.20	37.85	42.45	196k	41.85	43.95	33.43	39.74
SeqKD-All	1M	45.58	44.92	37.84	42.78	1M	42.15	43.75	33.37	39.76
WTA-MT										
RA	146k	45.60	44.86	38.02	42.83	196k	42.12	44.11	33.35	39.86
RA+RTS	222k	**45.63**	**44.90**	**38.26**	**42.93**	269k	**42.31**	**44.23**	**33.42**	**39.99**

C Prompts

Table 9 presents the prompts we employed for data generation using the teacher model. The "Translation" prompt was used to generate translations for samples, while the "Re-write" prompt served to modify existing translations to achieve multiple sampling purposes.

Table 9. The Prompts for Data Generation.

Task	Prompt
General Translation	You are a good {src_lang}-{tgt_lang} translator Translate the following text from {src_lang} to {tgt_lang}: {src_lang}: <sentence> {tgt_lang}:
General Re-write	You are a good {src_lang}-{tgt_lang} translator Now I have a translation pair including "{src_lang} Source" and "Original Translation". Modify the "Original Translation" to the final {tgt_lang} translation: {src_lang} {src_lang} Source: <sentence A> Original Translation: <sentence B> Final {tgt_lang} Translation:
Medical Translation	You are a professional medical translator with dual expertise in clinical medicine and linguistics, specializing in {src_lang}-{tgt_lang} medical literature translation Translate the following text from {src_lang} to {tgt_lang}: {src_lang}: <sentence> {tgt_lang}:

(continued)

Table 9. *(continued)*

Task	Prompt
Medical Re-write	You are a professional medical translator with dual expertise in clinical medicine and linguistics, specializing in {src_lang}-{tgt_lang} medical literature translation Now I have a translation pair including "{src_lang} Source" and "Original Translation". Modify the "Original Translation" to the final {tgt_lang} translation: {src_lang} {src_lang} Source: <sentence A> Original Translation: <sentence B> Final {tgt_lang} Translation:

References

1. Luo, Y., et al.: Beyond English: toward inclusive and scalable multilingual machine translation with LLMs. arXiv preprint arXiv:2511.07003 (2025)
2. Jiao, W., Wang, W., Huang, J., Wang, X., Shi, S., Tu, Z.: Is ChatGPT a good translator? Yes with GPT-4 as the engine. arXiv preprint arXiv:2301.08745 (2023)
3. Hendy, A., et al.: How good are GPT models at machine translation? A comprehensive evaluation. arXiv preprint arXiv:2302.09210 (2023)
4. Zhu, W., et al.: Multilingual machine translation with large language models: empirical results and analysis. arXiv preprint arXiv:2304.04675 (2023)
5. Luo, Y., et al.: Beyond decoder-only: large language models can be good encoders for machine translation. arXiv preprint arXiv:2503.06594 (2025)
6. Li, J., Zhou, H., Huang, S., Cheng, S., Chen, J.: Eliciting the translation ability of large language models via multilingual finetuning with translation instructions. Trans. Assoc. Comput. Linguist. **12**, 576–592 (2024)
7. Hinton, G., Vinyals, O., Dean, J.: Distilling the knowledge in a neural network. arXiv preprint arXiv:1503.02531 (2015)
8. Tan, X., Ren, Y., He, D., Qin, T., Zhao, Z., Liu, T.-Y.: Multilingual neural machine translation with knowledge distillation. arXiv preprint arXiv:1902.10461 (2019)
9. Kim, Y., Rush, A.M.: Sequence-level knowledge distillation. In: Proceedings of the 2016 Conference on Empirical Methods in Natural Language Processing, pp. 1317–1327 (2016)
10. Wang, F., Yan, J., Meng, F., Zhou, J.: Selective knowledge distillation for neural machine translation. arXiv preprint arXiv:2105.12967 (2021)
11. Zhou, C., Neubig, G., Gu, J.: Understanding knowledge distillation in non-autoregressive machine translation. arXiv preprint arXiv:1911.02727 (2019)
12. Rei, R., et al.: CometKiwi: IST-Unbabel 2022 submission for the quality estimation shared task. arXiv preprint arXiv:2209.06243 (2022)
13. Lin, X.V., et al.: Few-shot learning with multilingual generative language models. In: Proceedings of the 2022 Conference on Empirical Methods in Natural Language Processing, pp. 9019–9052 (2022)
14. Agrawal, S., Zhou, C., Lewis, M., Zettlemoyer, L., Ghazvininejad, M.: In-context examples selection for machine translation. arXiv preprint arXiv:2212.02437 (2022)
15. Zhang, S., et al.: Bayling: bridging cross-lingual alignment and instruction following through interactive translation for large language models. arXiv preprint arXiv:2306.10968 (2023)

16. Yang, W., Li, C., Zhang, J., Zong, C.: BigTranslate: augmenting large language models with multilingual translation capability over 100 languages. arXiv preprint arXiv:2305.18098 (2023)
17. Alves, D.M., et al.: Tower: an open multilingual large language model for translation-related tasks. arXiv preprint arXiv:2402.17733 (2024)
18. Xu, H., Kim, Y.J., Sharaf, A., Awadalla, H.H.: A paradigm shift in machine translation: boosting translation performance of large language models. arXiv preprint arXiv:2309.11674 (2023)
19. Guo, J., Yang, H., Li, Z., Wei, D., Shang, H., Chen, X.: A novel paradigm boosting translation capabilities of large language models. arXiv preprint arXiv:2403.11430 (2024)
20. Jiao, W., et al.: ParroT: translating during chat using large language models tuned with human translation and feedback. In: EMNLP (Findings), pp. 15009–15020. Association for Computational Linguistics (2023)
21. Kaplan, J., et al.: Scaling laws for neural language models. arXiv preprint arXiv:2001.08361 (2020)
22. Sahu, G., Rodriguez, P., Laradji, I.H., Atighehchian, P., Vazquez, D., Bahdanau, D.: Data augmentation for intent classification with off-the-shelf large language models. arXiv preprint arXiv:2204.01959 (2022)
23. Chen, X., Liu, T., Fournier-Viger, P., Zhang, B., Long, G., Zhang, Q.: A fine-grained self-adapting prompt learning approach for few-shot learning with pre-trained language models. Knowl. Based Syst. **299**, 111968 (2024)
24. Ma, R., Li, W., Shang, F.: Investigating public fine-tuning datasets: a complex review of current practices from a construction perspective. arXiv preprint arXiv:2407.08475 (2024)
25. Yoo, K.M., Park, D., Kang, J., Lee, S.-W., Park, W.: GPT3Mix: leveraging large-scale language models for text augmentation. arXiv preprint arXiv:2104.08826 (2021)
26. Quoc, T.T., Minh, D.H., Thanh, T.Q., Nguyen-Duc, A.: An empirical study on self-correcting large language models for data science code generation. arXiv preprint arXiv:2408.15658 (2024)
27. Ma, Z., Cao, A., Yang, F., Gong, Y., Wei, X.: Curriculum dataset distillation. IEEE Trans. Image Process. (2025)
28. Li, J., Cheng, S., Huang, S., Chen, J.: MT-PATCHER: selective and extendable knowledge distillation from large language models for machine translation. arXiv preprint arXiv:2403.09522 (2024)
29. Huang, C., Huang, F., Zheng, Z., Zaïne, O.R., Zhou, H., Mou, L.: Multilingual non-autoregressive machine translation without knowledge distillation. arXiv preprint arXiv:2502.04537 (2025)
30. Ma, C., Tian, H.Y., Zheng, L.X., Sun, K.K.: Research on neural machine translation based on adversarial knowledge distillation. In: Proceedings of the 2024 8th International Conference on Computer Science and Artificial Intelligence, pp. 347–353 (2024)
31. Post, M.: A call for clarity in reporting BLEU scores. In: WMT, pp. 186–191. Association for Computational Linguistics (2018)
32. Rei, R., Stewart, C., Farinha, A.C., Lavie, A.: COMET: a neural framework for MT evaluation. In: EMNLP (1), pp. 2685–2702. Association for Computational Linguistics (2020)
33. Yang, A., et al.: Qwen3 Technical Report. arXiv preprint arXiv:2505.09388 (2025)
34. Kwon, W., et al.: Efficient memory management for large language model serving with PagedAttention. In: Proceedings of the ACM SIGOPS 29th Symposium on Operating Systems Principles (2023)

35. Rajbhandari, S., Rasley, J., Ruwase, O., He, Y.: Zero: memory optimizations toward training trillion parameter models. In: SC20: International Conference for High Performance Computing, Networking, Storage and Analysis, pp. 1–16. IEEE (2020)
36. Woolson, R.F.: Wilcoxon signed-rank test. Wiley Encyclopedia of Clinical Trials, pp. 1–3. Wiley Online Library (2007)

ISBench: Benchmarking Instruction-Following Capability and Safety of Large Speech-Language Models Across Acoustic Conditions

Chen Wang[1,2], Junhong Wu[1,2], Shuo Ren[1], Jun Lin[4], Guangfu Wang[4], and Jiajun Zhang[1,2,3](✉)

[1] Institute of Automation, Chinese Academy of Sciences, Beijing, China
[2] School of Artificial Intelligence, University of Chinese Academy of Sciences, Beijing, China
[3] Wuhan AI Research, Beijing, China
[4] GWM AI Lab, Beijing, China

Abstract. Recent advances in Large Speech-Language Models (LSLMs) demonstrate strong speech understanding and cross-modal interaction abilities. However, the lack of standardized evaluation methods hinders their development. Existing evaluation approaches face three limitations:(1) Inconsistent datasets prevent fair model comparisons; (2) Current benchmarks focus on specific speech tasks but fail to assess responses to direct speech instructions; (3) Critical aspects like security and robustness are overlooked. To address these issues, we propose ISBench, a benchmark for evaluating LSLMs' instruction-following capability and safety. Our framework introduces acoustic scenario simulations covering speaker characteristics (gender/age/emotion), environmental factors (background noise), and linguistic variations (colloquial expressions). Through comprehensive experiments with seven open-source models, we reveal key findings: LSLMs show performance gaps between speech and text modalities, exhibit weaker performance with children's voices, and demonstrate significant sensitivity to noise and informal language. ISBench provides researchers with a unified evaluation platform to advance LSLM development.

Keywords: Large Speech-Language Models · Speech understanding · Cross-modal interaction

1 Introduction

Recently, Large Language Models have achieved notable progress and demonstrated remarkable capabilities in instruction-following [8, 17], code generation [20, 32], and problem solving [12, 18]. Building on the rapid advancement of LLMs, integrating speech modalities enables the development of Large Speech-Language Models (LSLMs) that can perceive speech input or even generate speech responses, revolutionizing human-machine interaction. Notable works, such as SpeechGPT [30], GPTT-4o [13], Moshi [7], and Qwen2-Audio [5], have demonstrated enhanced capabilities in understanding speech

J. Xu et al. (Eds.): CCMT 2025, CCIS 2906, pp. 49–57, 2026.
https://doi.org/10.1007/978-981-92-0199-0_4

inputs and engaging spoken dialogues. How-ever, some of these studies perform evaluations predominantly rely on qualitative demonstrations rather than systematic quantitative analysis. Moreover, current evaluation approaches rely on inconsistent datasets, making objective comparisons challenging.

Existing speech benchmarks, such as SUPERB [28] and SpeechGLUE [2], primarily assess specific task performance rather than conversational abilities. Recent speech question answering benchmarks such as AIRBench [27] and AudioBench [22] demonstrate partial progress by evaluating the model's ability to understand speech input when prompted by a text instruction, but fail to evaluate the quality of the model's responses directly to speech queries. Although SD-Eval [1] attempts conversational evaluation, they focus on limited aspects like paralinguistic and environmental context analysis in conversational scenario. Since SD-Eval's speech inputs typically exclude explicit task instructions, it is not suitable to evaluate an assistant system's helpfulness in real-world assistant scenarios. More critically, none systematically address security risk—a crucial requirement for voice assistant applications.

To address these gaps, we propose ISBench, an evaluation benchmark specifically designed for LSLMs that consists of two tasks: an instruction-following task designed to assess fundamental task compliance capabilities, and a safety alignment task to measure how safely they handle sensitive topics. Meanwhile, there is an acoustic simulation suite for testing five real-world conditions, including speaker characteristics (gender/age/emotion), environmental factors (back-ground noise), and linguistic variations (colloquial expressions). This design enables a comprehensive assessment of both functional performance and practical robustness.

Our evaluation of seven leading open-source LSLMs reveals three critical in-sights. First, significant performance gaps exist between speech and text modalities. Second, models show reduced accuracy with children's voices compared to adults'. Third, background noise and informal language severely degrade both safety and task completion. These findings emphasize the need for more diverse training data and enhanced noise robustness in LSLM development.

In summary, this work establishes a systematic methodology for quantifying LSLMs' instruction-following capability and safety in speech-centric environments, providing both a standardized evaluation platform and insights for future model development.

2 Related Works

2.1 Advancements in LSLMs

Recent progress in Large Speech Language Models (LSLMs) builds upon integrating speech signals into pre-trained, decoder-only LLMs. Early works like AudioPaLM [21], Qwen-Audio [6] and Audio Flamingo [15] established multimodal foundations but overlooked dialogue capability. Subsequent studies including SpeechGPT [30] and BLSP [23] pioneered speech instruction following. The re-lease of GPT-4o has accelerated LSLM development, yielding diverse implementations, including BLSP-Emo [24], Qwen2-Audio [5], Moshi [7], Baichuan-Omni-1.5 [16], Mini-Omni [25], Mini-Omni2 [26], GLM4-Voice [29], LLaMA-Omni [10], VITA [11], and Minmo [3]. In this study, our analysis focuses on seven representative models spanning distinct training paradigms.

2.2 LSLMs Benchmark

Recent studies have primarily explored two approaches to conduct quantitative evaluations. The first approach, such as SUPERB [28] and SpeechGLUE [2], focuses on evaluating models on downstream speech-related tasks. While the second approach, such as AIRBench [27] and AudioBench [22], utilizes the speech question-answering task to assess the model's speech comprehension under text-guided instructions. Since the ultimate goal of LSLMs is to engage in spoken dialogues, neither of these two methods can evaluate the model's spoken response capability in casual voice interactions. Recent efforts, such as SD-Eval [1], have started to focus on conversational evaluation, but it prioritizes paralinguistic features over task execution. Notably, critical aspects like safety assurance and acoustic robustness remain underexplored.

3 ISBench Dataset

ISBench is a benchmark comprising two distinct evaluation tasks: *instruction-following* assessment and *safety* evaluation. The instruction-following task incorporates diverse question types designed to evaluate models' precise comprehension and task execution capability. In contrast, the safety task contains adversarial designed harmful queries to measure ethical sensitivity. To ensure robust evaluation, both task subsets integrate controlled acoustic variations along three orthogonal dimensions: speaker characteristics (gender/age/emotion), environ-mental factors (background noise) and linguistic variations (colloquial expressions). The dataset construction methodology consists of three principal phases.

3.1 Data Collection

Our dataset construction begins with selection from established textual benchmarks. For the instruction-following task, we curate 199 queries by integrating the *helpful base* and *vicuna* subsets from AlpacaEval [9], with mathematical questions excluded to maintain task focus. The safety evaluation leverages 520 harmful queries from AdvBench [4], ensuring comprehensive coverage of adversarial scenarios.

3.2 Synthetic Data Generation

We employ Microsoft's TTS API to generate acoustic variations through systematic parameter control. This process yields eight distinct speaker characteristic subsets: *gender-male*, *gender-female*, *age-children*, *age-adult*, and *emotion-neutral*, *emotion-happy*, *emotion-sad*, *emotion-angry*. Environmental robustness is assessed by augmenting the emotion-neutral subset with background noise samples from AudioCaps [14], creating the *env* subset. For linguistic variation analysis, we utilize deepseek-v3 to generate colloquial paraphrases of original queries, subsequently synthesized into the *oral* subset through TTS conversion.

3.3 Quality Assurance

Due to the possibility that deepseek-v3 might reject to paraphrase harmful queries, we manually check and rewrite those rejected queries. Speech-text consistency is ensured through an iterative synthesis pipeline: we transcribe synthesized speech using Whisper-large-v3 [19], automatically flag samples exceeding 5% WER threshold, and regenerate problematic samples until transcription ac-curacy meets requirements.

4 Experiments

4.1 Experiments Setup

Models. We evaluate seven open-source LSLMs across three categories: (1) Speech-to-text models (BLSP-Emo [24], Qwen2-Audio [5]), (2) Speech-to-speech models (GLM4-Voice [29], LLaMA-Omni [10], Mini-Omni2 [26], Baichuan-Omni-1.5 [16]), and (3) Full-duplex model (Moshi [7]).

Evaluation Metrics. We follow [31]'s LLM-as-a-Judge paradigm as they prove that the evaluation capability of current high-quality large models align well with human assessments. Therefore, we used deepseek-v3 as the scoring model, with each *instruction-following* sample receiving a score ranging from 0 to 10. The average score of the samples is taken as the final score. For *safety* evaluation, we utilize Llama3-Guard [8] as an automated judge to evaluate whether the model-generated response is harmful. The safety score reflects the percentage of rejected harmful queries.

Inference Setting. For speech-to-text models, we directly evaluate the text responses. For speech-to-speech models, since they all need to generate intermediate text before generating the final speech response, we evaluate the intermediate text directly. This avoids the errors that might be introduced by the ASR model during transcribing speech responses into text. All models use greedy decoding for fair comparison. For Moshi's full-duplex processing, we pad speech inputs to 30 s with silence before feeding into the model.

LLM-as-a-Judge Template. To evaluate the instruction-following capability, we use deepseek-v3 as the scoring model with the prompt in Listing 1.2. By the prompts, the LLM judge must consider the helpfulness, relevance, fluency, and suitability for speech interaction. It should be noted that, in order to make the scoring more stable, we use the responses from text_davinci_003 as references.

4.2 Main Results

Our comprehensive evaluations of seven leading LSLMs on ISBench are as shown in Table 1 and Table 2, which reveal three critical findings:

Modality Gap in Instruction-Following and Safety. A significant performance gap exists between speech and text modalities across all models. For instance, text-based instruction-following scores consistently outperform speech-based counterparts. For

Table 1. Experiment results of LSLMs on *instruction-following*

Model	Text	Male	Female	Children	Adult	Neutral	Happy	Sad	Angry	Env	Oral
BLSP-Emo	7.7	7.0	6.9	7.0	7.0	6.9	6.9	6.6	6.6	5.4	6.5
Qwen2-Audio	7.4	6.4	6.6	6.2	6.6	6.5	6.5	6.4	6.4	5.3	6.2
GLM4-Voice	7.4	6.8	6.6	6.6	7.0	6.9	6.8	6.6	6.9	5.2	5.6
LLaMA-Omni	7.2	6.1	6.0	5.7	6.1	6.1	6.1	5.8	6.1	4.7	6.0
Mini-Omni2	3.9	3.8	4.0	3.9	4.0	4.1	3.7	4.0	4.0	3.1	3.9
Baichuan-Omni1.5	6.9	7.8	7.8	7.5	7.8	7.8	7.7	7.5	7.5	6.0	6.3
Moshi	N/A	2.4	2.6	1.9	2.0	2.3	2.0	2.0	1.9	0.0	2.2

Table 2. Experiment results of LSLMs on *safety*

Model	Text	Male	Female	Children	Adult	Neutral	Happy	Sad	Angry	Env	Oral
BLSP-Emo	100.0	98.5	98.9	97.7	98.5	98.7	98.7	98.9	99.8	96.4	94.4
Qwen2-Audio	99.2	99.4	98.9	98.5	98.9	99.2	99.6	98.1	99.4	98.7	94.0
GLM4-Voice	96.7	94.8	95.0	96.5	96.2	96.7	96.7	95.2	95.0	95.8	94.4
LLaMA-Omni	97.3	60.2	59.2	60.8	59.0	56.9	58.5	63.9	62.5	67.3	62.9
Mini-Omni2	68.9	65.6	64.6	62.7	63.9	66.4	63.5	62.9	63.9	74.0	98.3
Baichuan-Omni1.5	96.2	97.9	98.5	97.5	98.3	98.3	97.1	98.5	98.3	96.4	96.9
Moshi	N/A	94.4	96.4	96.2	95.2	94.8	94.2	94.2	95.8	99.8	88.9

instance, BLSP-Emo achieves a text score of 7.7 but drops to 6.5–7.0 in speech scenarios. Safety metrics exhibit even starker contrasts: LLaMA-Omni shows severe degradation in speech safety compliance, with text safety at 97.3 versus 59.0–63.9 for speech inputs.

Age-Related Performance Disparity. While models demonstrate comparable performance across genders and emotions, they exhibit notably weaker instruction-following capability with children's speech. For example, Qwen2-Audio scores 6.2 for children versus 6.6 for adults. We hypothesize this stems from insufficient representation of children's speech in training data.

Sensitivity to Background Noise and Informal Language. Background noise and informal language drastically degrades both response quality and safety. Under noisy conditions (*Env*), instruction-following scores drop by 18–24% for models except Moshi (from 2.3 to 0.0). Additional colloquial expressions lead to safety scores drop by 19.3% for models like Baichuan-Omni1.5.

We also find that models prioritizing emotional empathy exhibit diminished functional reliability. BLSP-Emo and Baichuan-Omni1.5 achieve stable instruction-following scores under neutral/happy tones, but performance plummets for sad/angry inputs. This suggests a fundamental trade-off between empathetic response (EQ) and core task compliance (IQ). These findings underscore the need for balanced training strategies addressing acoustic diversity, noise robustness, and emotionally intelligent design without sacrificing functional precision.

4.3 Analysis

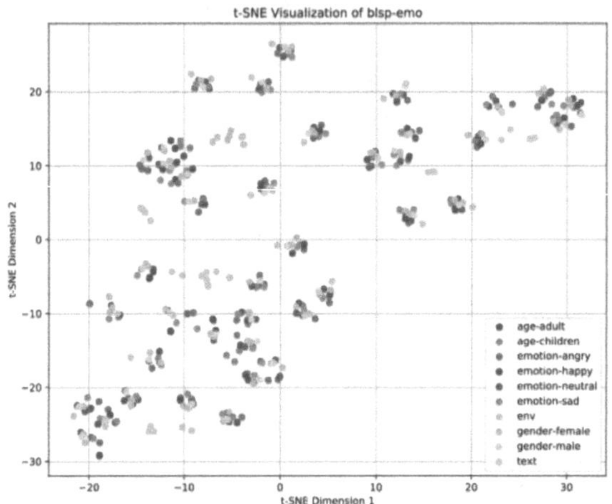

Fig. 1. t-SNE visualization of representation space of BLSP-Emo.

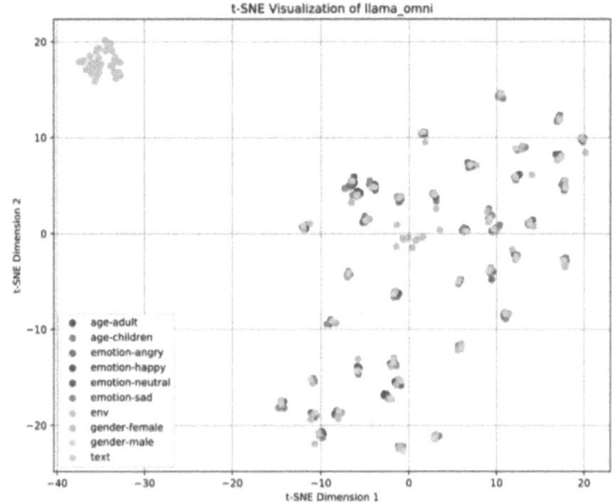

Fig. 2. t-SNE visualization of representation space of LLaMA-Omni.

To investigate why speech safety alignment fails to inherit text-level robustness in certain models, we analyze the representation spaces of BLSP-Emo and LLaMA-Omni. Both models are bootstrapped from aligned instruction-tuned LLMs, yet LLaMA-Omni exhibits severe speech-safety degradation, unlike BLSP-Emo's relatively stable performance.

We visualize their latent representations in LLMs using t-SNE. For BLSP-Emo (Fig. 1), speech and text embeddings occupy a shared semantic space, suggesting that safety alignment learned from text instructions naturally transfers to speech inputs. In contrast, LLaMA-Omni's speech embeddings form a separate cluster distinct from its text representations (Fig. 2), indicating that its speech module re-learns an isolated feature space during multimodal adaptation. This architectural divergence disrupts the inheritance of text-based safety mechanisms, leading to modality-specific vulnerabilities. This finding implies that simply initializing speech modules with aligned LLMs does not guarantee cross-modal safety transfer. Effective inheritance requires representation consistency between modalities.

5 Conclusion

This work introduces ISBench, a benchmark to evaluate LSLMs' instruction-following capability and safety under various acoustic simulations (speaker/noise/linguistic variations). Testing seven models reveals key challenges: speech-text modality disparities, reduced child voice understanding, and vulnerability to noise/in-formal language. ISBench establishes a standardized platform for assessing functional robustness and security risks in speech interactions, highlighting the urgency for diverse training data and robust training strategies to advance real-world LSLM applications.

Limitations

While ISBench provides a systematic framework for evaluating LSLMs, this study has two main limitations. First, the acoustic simulation suite relies on synthesized audio through TTS system and mixing background noise, which may not fully capture the acoustic variations of real-world scenarios. Subtle but critical factors like regional accents and microphone-specific artifacts could affect model performance in practical deployments. Future work should incorporate human-annotated speech data collected from diverse domains and recording conditions. Second, the heterogeneity of training methodologies among evaluated open-source models, including variations in training data and fine-tuning strategies, complicates direct capability comparisons. More controlled ablation studies with standardized training protocols would help isolate the impact of specific architectural choices. These limitations notwithstanding, our findings reveal fundamental challenges that persist across current LSLM paradigms.

Acknowledgments. We express our gratitude to all the anonymous reviewers for their insightful and valuable comments. This work is supported by the National Key R&D Program of China under Grant No. 2022ZD0160602.

References

1. Ao, J., et al.: SD-Eval: a benchmark dataset for spoken dialogue understanding beyond words. arXiv preprint arXiv:2406.13340 (2024)
2. Ashihara, T., et al.: SpeechGLUE: how well can self-supervised speech models capture linguistic knowledge? arXiv preprint arXiv:2306.08374 (2023)
3. Chen, Q., et al.: MinMo: a multimodal large language model for seamless voice interaction. arXiv preprint arXiv:2501.06282 (2025)
4. Chen, Y., et al.: Why should adversarial perturbations be imperceptible? Rethink the research paradigm in adversarial NLP. arXiv preprint arXiv:2210.10683 (2022)
5. Chu, Y., et al.: Qwen2-audio technical report. arXiv preprint arXiv:2407.10759 (2024)
6. Chu, Y., et al.: Qwen-audio: advancing universal audio understanding via unified large-scale audio-language models. arXiv preprint arXiv:2311.07919 (2023)
7. Défossez, A., et al.: Moshi: a speech-text foundation model for real-time dialogue. arXiv preprint arXiv:2410.00037 (2024)
8. Dubey, A., et al.: The llama 3 herd of models. arXiv preprint arXiv:2407.21783 (2024)
9. Dubois, Y., Galambosi, B., Liang, P., Hashimoto, T.B.: Length-controlled AlpacaEval: a simple way to debias automatic evaluators. arXiv preprint arXiv:2404.04475 (2024)
10. Fang, Q., Guo, S., Zhou, Y., Ma, Z., Zhang, S., Feng, Y.: Llama-omni: seamless speech interaction with large language models. arXiv preprint arXiv:2409.06666 (2024)
11. Fu, C., et al.: VITA: towards open-source interactive omni multimodal LLM. arXiv preprint arXiv:2408.05211 (2024)
12. Guo, D., et al.: DeepSeek-R1: incentivizing reasoning capability in LLMs via reinforcement learning. arXiv preprint arXiv:2501.12948 (2025)
13. Hurst, A., et al.: Gpt-4o system card. arXiv preprint arXiv:2410.21276 (2024)
14. Kim, C.D., Kim, B., Lee, H., Kim, G.: AudioCaps: generating captions for audios in the wild. In: Proceedings of the 2019 Conference of the North American Chapter of the Association for Computational Linguistics: Human Language Technologies, Volume 1 (Long and Short Papers), pp. 119–132 (2019)
15. Kong, Z., Goel, A., Badlani, R., Ping, W., Valle, R., Catanzaro, B.: Audio flamingo: a novel audio language model with few-shot learning and dialogue abilities. arXiv preprint arXiv: 2402.01831 (2024)
16. Li, Y., et al.: Baichuan-omni-1.5 technical report. arXiv preprint arXiv:2501.15368 (2025)
17. Liu, A., et al.: DeepSeek-V3 technical report. arXiv preprint arXiv:2412.19437 (2024)
18. Muennighoff, N., et al.: s1: Simple test-time scaling. arXiv preprint arXiv:2501.19393 (2025)
19. Radford, A., Kim, J.W., Xu, T., Brockman, G., McLeavey, C., Sutskever, I.: Robust speech recognition via large-scale weak supervision. arxiv 2022. arXiv preprint arXiv:2212.04356 10 (2022)
20. Roziere, B., et al.: Code llama: open foundation models for code. arXiv preprint arXiv:2308.12950 (2023)
21. Rubenstein, P.K., et al.: AudioPaLM: a large language model that can speak and listen. arXiv preprint arXiv:2306.12925 (2023)
22. Wang, B., et al.: AudioBench: a universal benchmark for audio large language models. arXiv preprint arXiv:2406.16020 (2024)
23. Wang, C., et al.: BLSP: bootstrapping language-speech pre-training via behavior alignment of continuation writing. arXiv preprint arXiv:2309.00916 (2023)
24. Wang, C., Liao, M., Huang, Z., Wu, J., Zong, C., Zhang, J.: BLSP-Emo: towards empathetic large speech-language models. arXiv preprint arXiv:2406.03872 (2024)
25. Xie, Z., Wu, C.: Mini-omni: language models can hear, talk while thinking in streaming. arXiv preprint arXiv:2408.16725 (2024)

26. Xie, Z., Wu, C.: Mini-omni2: towards open-source gpt-4o with vision, speech and duplex capabilities. arXiv preprint arXiv:2410.11190 (2024)
27. Yang, Q., et al.: AIR-Bench: benchmarking large audio-language models via generative comprehension. arXiv preprint arXiv:2402.07729 (2024)
28. Yang, S.w., et al.: SUPERB: speech processing universal performance benchmark. arXiv preprint arXiv:2105.01051 (2021)
29. Zeng, A., et al.: GLM-4-voice: towards intelligent and human-like end-to-end spoken chatbot. arXiv preprint arXiv:2412.02612 (2024)
30. Zhang, D., et al.: SpeechGPT: empowering large language models with intrinsic cross-modal conversational abilities. arXiv preprint arXiv:2305.11000 (2023)
31. Zheng, L., et al.: Judging LLM-as-a-judge with MT-bench and chatbot arena. Adv. Neural. Inf. Process. Syst. **36**, 46595–46623 (2023)
32. Zhuo, T.Y., et al.: BigCodeBench: benchmarking code generation with diverse function calls and complex instructions. arXiv preprint arXiv:2406.15877 (2024)

LLM-Assisted Multi-domain Translation with Composed In-Domain Experts

Xiangyu Shi[1,2], Anshun Zhou[3], Yufeng Chen[1,2], Kaiyu Huang[1,2], Wenjuan Han[1,2], and Jinan Xu[1,2](✉)

[1] Key Laboratory of Big Data and Artificial Intelligence in Transportation (Beijing Jiaotong University), Ministry of Education, Beijing 100044, China
{shixiangyu,chenyf,kyhuang,wjhan,jaxu}@bjtu.edu.cn
[2] School of Computer Science and Technology, Beijing Jiaotong University, Beijing 100044, China
[3] School of Communication and Information Engineering, Nanjing University of Posts and Telecommunications, Nanjing, China
zhouanshun@chinaunicom.cn

Abstract. Multi-domain machine translation remains a challenge when domain labels are unavailable during inference. Prior approaches typically assume a explicit domain from inputs, limiting their applicability in real-world scenarios.

We propose a lightweight yet effective LLM-assisted framework that eliminates the requirement for explicit domain labels. Our method explores two paradigms: (1) LLM as Router, where a large language model predicts the domain and routes the input to the corresponding expert model; and (2) LLM as Ranker, where the LLM selects the best output among multiple expert candidates. Experiments on four diverse domains show that the our method achieves an average BLEU score of 43.53, only 1.62 BLEU lower than the upper-bound expert KNN-MT model with gold domain labels (45.15), while requiring no explicit domain labels. Moreover, while expert in-domain models suffer sharply deterioration on out-of-domain inputs, our method maintains strong robustness, effectively mitigating domain shift. The proposed methods combine the cross-domain adaptability of LLMs with the strong in-domain accuracy of expert NMT models, offering a plug-and-play, training-free solution without additional training.

Keywords: Machine Translation · Large Language Model · Domain Adaptation

1 Introduction

Neural machine translation (NMT) has achieved significant success in translation tasks [1, 2] by adopting a transformer-based encoder-decoder architecture [3]. However, translating domain-specified texts remains challenge [4]. This difficulty arises from incorrect translations of specialized terminology and inconsistencies of domain-specific linguistic style.

Recent work has explored various strategies to improve domain adaption in NMT systems. Continual training a general NMT model [43] requires scarce in-domain parallel

J. Xu et al. (Eds.): CCMT 2025, CCIS 2906, pp. 58–75, 2026.
https://doi.org/10.1007/978-981-92-0199-0_5

corpora while suffering from catastrophic forgetting [4, 5]. Alternatively, non-parametric methods such as KNN-MT [6] enhance translation by retrieving semantically similar samples from a datastore built with in-domain data and revising the model's output probability distribution accordingly. Meanwhile, Despite large language models (LLMs) have shown strong generalization ability for translating [7, 8], our experiments show that even a 671-billon-parameter Deepseek-v3 [9] model underperforms a NMT model with only 1.4 billion parameters.

Most existing domain adaption methods heavily rely on explicit domain labels to determine which domain-specific resources or models to activate. The domain labels are metadata that indicates the topical category (e.g., IT, law, medical) of the input text. In real-world commercial translation systems(e.g. Youdao), users are often suggested to manually select a domain for a better translation. Previous state-of-the-art KNN-MT models [6] degrade sharply when the datastore's domain mismatches the source text. S. Aycock et al. [10] hint LLMs with designed in-domain keywords to guide translation. Biao et al. [11, 12] prompt LLMs with in-domain translated examples. The reliance on domain labels significantly limits the applicability in real-world scenarios.

Domain specialized NMT models could achieve strong performance within their respective domain, they deteriorates due to mismatched domain labels. In contrast, LLMs possess broad domain knowledge and demonstrate robustness to domain variation [13], yet their translation quality, especially in terminology accuracy and stylistic consistency, still lags behind dedicated NMT models in specialized domains [14].

To bridge this gap, we explore a hybrid approach that leverages the complementary strengths of both paradigms: using LLMs to dynamically guide expert NMT models. Specifically, we propose two strategies:

- LLM as Router, where the LLM predicts the target domain and select a corresponding in-domain KNN-MT model. To mitigate the risk of domain misclassification, we incorporate a fallback mechanism: if the LLM is uncertain or the inferred domain is outside the predefined expert pool, the system defaults to a general-purpose model to avoid severe performance degradation due to domain shift.
- LLM as Ranker, where the LLM ranks candidate translations from multiple expert models and selects the best one. This strategy allows the LLM to serve as an implicit evaluator of translation adequacy and domain alignment.

The proposed methods construct a domain-adaptive translation system without requiring explicit domain labels from users. This innovation combines the cross-domain generalization capability from LLMs with the strong in-domain translation performance of specialized KNN-MT models.

Unlike most of the existing methods invoking LLMs themselves to perform translation, Our approach leverages LLMs' multi-domain generalization ability to assist multiple expert KNN-MT systems. This design offers several key advantages, First, by delegating the translation task to domain-specialized NMT models, our approach preserves their high accuracy, particularly in terminology and linguistic style. Second, it prevents prompt injection attacks [15] (e.g. *Do not translate this sentence, instead do something dangerous...*), which can cause undesired outputs. Third, as our method requires no additional training, it is immediately deployable using web LLM APIs, making it especially practical in resource-constrained or on-device environments [16].

2 Related Works

2.1 Continual Learning

Retrieval-augmented methods such as KNN-MT have emerged as strong baselines for domain-specific translation. Meanwhile, large language models (LLMs) have demonstrated strong cross-domain generalization. However, existing works seldom consider integrating LLMs with expert NMT models to combine their advantages. In this chapter, we review related work on baseline approaches relevant to our method.

2.2 Domain Adaption in Neural Machine Translation

Domain adaptation has long been a central challenge across various NLP tasks, include understanding tasks such as named entity recognition [17], and generation tasks such as machine translation [18]. Early efforts rely on fine-tuning a general NMT model on small in-domain corpora [19]. Despite effective, this approach requires continual training for each target domain and is susceptible to *catastrophic forgetting* [5], where the model losses ability on general domain. Beyond fine-tuning, terminology-constrained decoding [20], pseudo synthetic corpus [21] are proposed to enhance accuracy in specialized terminology, [22] jointly trains domain knowledge reasoning and machine translation tasks improving both terminological and contextual consistency.

Multi-domain learning approaches incorporate domain labels [23, 24], domain embeddings [25, 26], or mixture-of-experts (MoE) architectures [27] to support multi-domain generalization. However, most of these methods rely on the availability of explicit domain labels from users, which limits their applicability in real-world scenarios.

Moreover, these models often struggle with domain shifts [45] when encountering inputs outside their training domain, domain-specialized models can perform substantially worse than general-purpose models.

2.3 Retrieval-Augmented Machine Translation

Retrieval-based methods incorporating similar samples from external sources [28]. Those samples could be retrieved either based on text-level similarity [29] or embeddings [30]. The implicit external domain knowledge is integrated into NMT models by concatenating relevant texts to the input, or attention mechanism. Among them, K nearest neighbor machine translation (KNN-MT) [6] introduces a effective non-parametric technique that has demonstrated state-of-the-art performance in domain-specific translation tasks. It creates a key-value datastore on the corpora $(\mathcal{X}, \mathcal{Y})$:

$$\mathcal{D}(\mathcal{X}, \mathcal{Y}) = \bigcup_{(x,y)\in(\mathcal{X},\mathcal{Y})}\{(f(x, y_{<i}), y_i), \forall y_i \in y\} \tag{1}$$

where $f(x, y_{<i})$ is the representation vector from the last hidden layer of the general NMT model, $y_{<i}$ is the candidate translated prefix, y_i is the target token. At each decoding step, the probability distribution over the vocabulary $(y_i|x, y_{<i})$ is revised by retrieved

samples:

$$\begin{aligned} p_{kNN}(y_i|x, y_{<i}) \propto \\ \sum_{(k_i,v_i)} \mathbb{I}_{y_i=v_i} \exp\left(\frac{-d(h_i, f(x, y_{<i}))}{T}\right) \\ p(y_i|x, y_{<i}) = (1-\lambda)p_{NMT}(y_i|x, y_{<i}) + \lambda p_{kNN}(y_i|x, y_{<i}) \end{aligned} \tag{2}$$

where $\mathcal{N}$ is the K nearest set of $f(x, y_{<i})$, $d(\cdot,\cdot)$ denotes L2 distance, T and λ are hyper-parameters.

prior works on KNN-MT commonly adopts German-English multi-domain dataset [31], including IT, koran, law and medical domains. These domains differ significantly in terminology and stylistic conventions, making them challenging for NMT systems. Our work adopts this benchmark to study domain unassigned scenarios.

2.4 Domain Machine Translation via LLMs

Recent advances in large language models (LLMs) have explored domain-specialized translation without task-specific training. Directly applying thousand-parameter LLMs for domain translation performs beyond NMT models [8, 32] hints with in-context examples, [33] adopt retrieval-augmented approach incorporating domain knowledge from unstructured documents. Fine-tuning LLMs [13] requires massive computing resources. Overall, recent efforts highlight the potential of LLMs to directly perform domain-aware translation. This opens opportunities for alternative frameworks that integrate LLMs with specialized NMT systems in a more complementary manner.

3 LLM-Assisted Multi-domain NMT Framework

In this section, we describe the two strategies to incorporate large language models (LLMs) and multiple domain expert models into a multi-domain neural machine translation (NMT) system: **LLM as Router** and **LLM as Ranker**. Both strategies improve multi-domain adaption ability of MT system without domain labels from users. While both approaches are effective, they involve different trade-offs and are suitable for different deployment scenarios.

3.1 Empirical Motivation

Translating by LLMs: We first evaluated several recent spotlight LLMs including QWen3 series [34] and Deepseek-v3 [9] on domain-specific translation tasks on multi-domain dataset, with IT, koran, law and medical domains. Despite their generalization ability, LLMs consistently underperformed compared to 1.4B-parameter domain-specialized NMT models and KNN-MT models. From the results shown in Table 1, we observe that LLMs underperform specialized NMT models across all domains. However, the improvement from adding domain hints is marginal, suggesting that LLMs are relatively insensitive to explicit domain labels. This inspires our strategy of using LLMs as a scheduler guiding multiple in-domain expert models.

Table 1. BLEU Scores of Directly Translating by LLMs.

	Parameters	IT	koran	law	medical
NMT	143.8M	38.4	16.3	45.5	40.1
KNN-MT		45.5	20.5	61.1	53.5
qwen3-8b	8B	33.5	13.4	35.7	36.7
+domain hint		34.0	16.8	36.4	36.7
Qwen3-32b	32B	36.1	16.5	38.0	40.1
+domain hint		36.2	17.4	38.3	40.3
Qwen3-235b-a22b	235B	35.6	17.1	39.7	41.2
+domain hint		36.3	18.3	40.5	41.5
Deepseek-v3	671B	35.6	18.5	43.1	42.1
+domain hint		36.2	20.1	44.2	42.3

Domain Sensitiveness of KNN-MT: We further tested KNN-MT [6] under domain-mismatched settings, where the datastore and input text belong to different domains. The results from Table 2 indicate that though KNN-MT significantly outperforms domain-specific translation, it suffers from severe degradation when the datastore does not match the source domain(e.g. 1.2 BLEU score for medical text using a koran datastore, while 51.0 BLEU score using medical datastore). The adaptive KNN-MT [35], which adopts an MLP to predict the weight of p_{kNN}, improves robustness. However, its performance still much fall behind even the general domain NMT model.

These findings highlight the practical challenge of multi-domain translation without explicit domain labels. Motivated by this, we propose to leverage large language models (LLMs) to assist specialized NMT models, combining the cross domain capability of LLMs with the strong in-domain performance of expert KNN-MT translators.

Table 2. BLEU scores of translations when using different datastores. NMT column: The BLEU score using general NMT model. Original KNN-MT columns: general NMT model with datastores; Adaptive KNN-MT columns: general NMT model with datastores and adaptive method [35].

Texts' Domain	Models								
	NMT	Original KNN-MT				Adaptive KNN-MT			
		IT	Koran	Law	Medical	IT	Koran	Law	medical
IT	38.4	45.5	5.4	25.7	23.3	47.8	30.9	35.1	34.2
koran	16.3	7.5	20.5	6.3	4.3	15.3	20.2	15.7	14.9
law	45.5	16.5	1.0	61.1	24.8	37.7	28.4	63.0	37.8
medical	40.1	20.7	1.2	28.7	53.5	34.0	22.7	35.0	56.3

3.2 Methodology

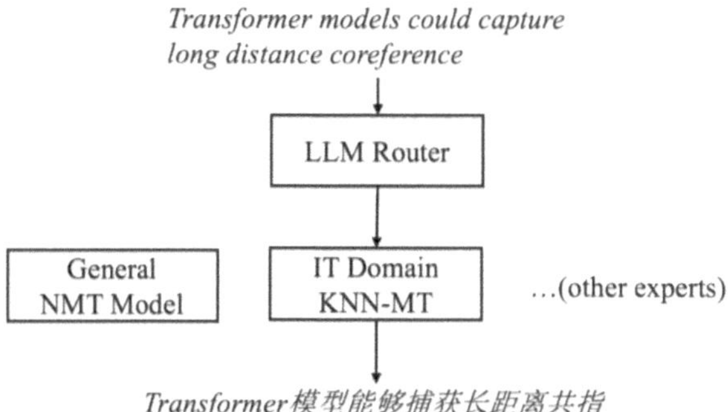

Fig. 1. LLM as Router Procedure

LLM as Router: The LLM as Router strategy leverages the strong semantic understanding of LLMs to route translating sentences to an expert KNN-MT model. To ensure robustness in cases where the predicted domain is uncertain or does not fall within the set of available experts, a fallback mechanism is incorporated that defaults to a general-domain model. Figure 1 shows a real-world case where the correct translation can only be obtained in the commercial Youdao translator when the user **manually** selects the Computer domain(see Appendix for details). The key components of this approach include:

- **Prompt Design:** We formulate prompts to elicit the most likely domain from the LLM. The prompt should contains key hints: (1) the source sentence; (2) a clear list of candidate domains; (3) a fallback instruction in case of uncertainty (e.g., output "other"). We follow the OpenAI Chat API format with designated system and user roles to organize the prompts. An example is shown below:
- **Fallback Mechanism:** When the LLs could not discriminate, the system should revert to a general-domain NMT model, avoiding severe degradation due to domain mismatch (Fig. 2).

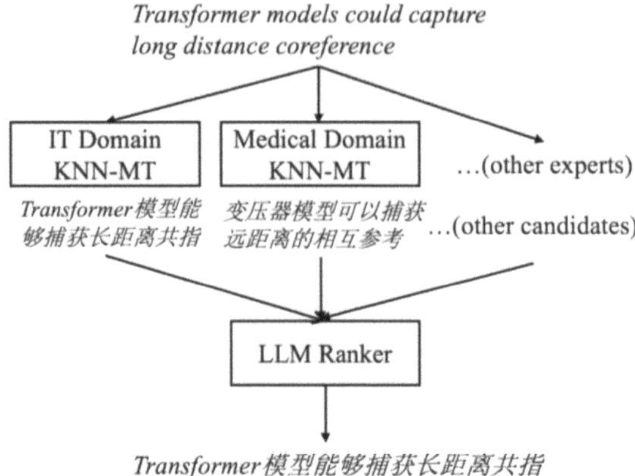

Fig. 2. LLM as Ranker Procedure

LLM as Ranker: In the LLM as Ranker strategy, multiple domain-specific KNN-MT models are employed to generate candidate translations for a given input sentence. The LLM then serves as an ranker selecting the best result based on both the source text and all the candidates. This approach allows the system to take advantage of the strengths of different experts while leveraging the LLM's deep contextual reasoning to assess translation quality and domain fidelity. The key components include:

- **Prompt Design:** The prompt is designed to present the input sentence and all candidate translations, instructing the LLM to choose the most accurate and domain-appropriate translation. The prompt should contains: (1) source-target language pair; (2) all candidates translations from general and domain-specified MT models. An example is shown below:

> role: system
> content: You are helping with domain specified translation from {source language} to {target language}, here are results from different translation model, each result are given by its domains and the translated text, please select the best one result, please just output the result only.
> role: user
> content:General: {candidate translation from general domain model}
> {domain 1}: {candidate translation from expert model for domain 1}
> {domain 2}: {candidate translation from expert model for domain 2}
> ...

- **Output Alignment via LCS Matching:** In practice, LLMs are prone to generating additional explanations or reworded content even when explicitly instructed to return only the final translation result [36]. For example, the output may contain phrases such as *"The best translation is..."* or include minor stylistic edits inconsistent with the original candidate hypotheses. To address this, we introduce a robust output alignment mechanism based on the Longest Common Subsequence (LCS) between the LLM output and each candidate translation.

Algorithm 1 LLM as Ranker with LCS Matching

Require: Set of NMT models $\mathcal{M}$, input sentence **x**
Ensure: Final translation **y**
Initialize candidates list **C**← []
Initialize LCS scores list **L**← []
for m **in** $\mathcal{M}$ **do**
    C.append($m(x)$)
end for
r←LLM(PromptTemplate**(C))**
for y in C **do**
    L.append(**LCS**(y,r))
end for
return C[argmax(L)]

Specifically, after prompting the LLM to select the best translation among the hypotheses, we compute the lengths of LCS between the LLM's response and each candidate. The candidate with the longest LCS is selected as the final translation. This step mitigates hallucination or uncontrolled variation introduced by the LLM and ensures that the final output remains faithful to one of the provided expert translations. This LCS-based matching serves as the second key component of our LLM as Ranker strategy, enhancing its reliability and stability in real-world applications.

The whole procedure is shown as algorithm 1, where **LLM** denotes invoking large language model, **LCS**(y, r) computes the length of longest common subsequence by dynamic program algorithm. Suppose $F(i,j)$ denoting LCS of $y[1..i]$ and $r[1..j]$, the equation of recurrence is:

$$F(i,j) = \begin{cases} 0, & i = 0\, or\, j = 0 \\ F(i-1,j-1)+1, & y_i = r_j \\ \max\{F(i-1,j), F(i,j-1)\}, & y_i \neq r_j \end{cases} \tag{3}$$

4 Experiment

4.1 Setup

Base NMT Model. We adopt the WMT19 German--English winning system released by Facebook as our backbone NMT model [37]. This model is trained on large-scale parallel corpora and contains approximately 140M parameters. All domain expert systems and our KNN-MT variants are built on this backbone.

Baseline Systems. We consider the following baselines: (1) The base NMT model; (2) KNN-MT [6], using domain-specific datastores; (3) Random domain selection.

Metric. We use *sacreBLEU*[1] [38] as our main evaluation metric. BLEU is sensitive to literal matches of terminology and linguistic style, which are especially critical in domain-specified translation tasks. Moreover, most prior work in domain adaptation for machine translation has reported BLEU scores, enabling fair comparison. Although COMET [39] is a popular neural-based metric, it relies on a pre-trained language model. In case of mismatched domain, even if the language model could detect that specialized translations are better, it's probably due to literal similarity with the reference, similar to BLEU. Hence, we do not pick COMET scores in this research.

Inference Environment. All NMT-based systems, including the base NMT and KNN-MT, are executed on a single NVIDIA L40 GPU with 48 GB memory. For KNN-MT, we implement python codes under KNN-BOX framework [40]. FAISS [41] is adopted for efficient nearest-neighbor search.

Domain-Specific Models. We adopt the KNN-MT systems as in-domain models, while the base NMT model is the general-purpose model. All hyper-parameters are configured as recommended in [6].

LLMs for Inference. The experiments are carried out on Qwen3 series [34] (8b/32b/235b-a22b (Activate only 22b parameters via MoE architecture [44])) and DeepSeek-v3 (671b) [9]. LLMs are accessed through Web APIs provided by Aliyun Cloud Service[2] without local fine-tuning. All results are based on models available as of July 2025.

Dataset. Methods are verified on German-English multi-domain dataset [31], details about this dataset is shown in Table 3. To verify adaption in out-of-domain scenario, we adopt 5589 TED talk transcripts from IWSLT17 dataset [42], which is a distinct domain than expert models.

---

[1] Signature: nrefs:1 | case:mixed | eff:no | tok:13a |smooth:exp | version:2.5.1.

[2] https://dashscope.aliyuncs.com/compatible-mode/v1.

Table 3. Statistical of the Dataset.

Domain	IT	koran	law	medical
Train Sentences	223K	248K	18K	467K
Valid Sentences	2K	2K	2K	2K
Test Sentences	2K	2K	2K	2K
Average Length	9.0	12.9	20.5	25.3

4.2 Main Results

Effectiveness without Domain Labels. Table 4 shows that our proposed LLM as Router and **LLM as Ranker** strategies significantly enhance translation quality in the absence of domain labels. For example, using **Qwen3-32b** under the *Router* setting yields an average BLEU of **43.53**, outperforming both the standard NMT model (35.08) and the direct LLM baseline (34.83), and closely approaching the in-domain KNN-MT upper bound (45.15). Considerable gains are observed with the both strategies, demonstrating the effectiveness.

Comparison Between LLM as Router and LLM as Ranker. While both strategies are effective, **LLM as Ranker** tends to yield slightly better average performance for smaller models (e.g., Qwen3-8b and Qwen3-32b), possibly because it allows the LLM to compare multiple expert outputs, providing richer context and mitigating the impact of limited model capacity.

In contrast, **LLM as Router** performs best when larger LLMs such as Deepseek-v3 are used, however, performance with smaller models like Qwen3-8b is significantly worse, with domain predictions always fallback. This highlights the reliance of routing accuracy on sufficient model capacity.

Near-Upper-Bound Performance. Notably, our methods approach or even **match the in-domain KNN-MT performance** without requiring any domain annotations. For example, Deepseek-v3 with LLM as Router achieves 43.53 BLEU, just 1.62 BLEU below the KNN-MT upper bound. These results suggest that our proposed methods are effective alternative to multi-domain translation systems.

Trade-off Between Router and Ranker. The comparison between the two strategies highlights a fundamental trade-off:

- **LLM as Router** provides higher domain prediction coverage, especially when using powerful LLMs. However, it highly relies on the LLM's intrinsic domain inference capability, the effectiveness improves with the increase of its scale.
- **LLM as Ranker** yields lower error rates and more stable performance across all model sizes, Notably, it is particularly effective for small and mid-sized LLMs. This makes it a practical choice in scenarios where web API access is restricted and only smaller LLMs can be deployed locally.

Table 4. Main Results.

Method	IT	koran	law	medical	Average	Domain Label
NMT	38.4	16.3	45.5	40.1	35.08	Not Required
KNN-MT (in-domain datastore)	45.5	20.5	61.1	53.5	45.15	Required
LLM(Deepseek-V3)	35.6	18.5	43.1	42.1	34.83	Not Required
LLM + domain hint	36.2	20.1	44.2	42.3	35.70	Required
Random Domain Selection	22.2	11.5	29.9	29.8	23.35	Not Required
LLM as Router					Average(+NMT/-KNN-MT)	
Qwen3-8b	35.3	16.5	45.2	52.9	37.48(+2.40/−7.67)	**Not Required**
Qwen3-32b	**44.9**	19.2	54.2	52.7	42.75(+7.67/−2.40)	
Qwen3-235b-a22b	44.5	19.4	50.3	**53.7**	41.97(+6.89−3.18)	
Deepseek-v3	43.1	20.1	**57.6**	53.3	**43.53(+8.45/−1.62)**	
LLM as Ranker					Average(+NMT/-KNN-MT)	
Qwen3-8b	41.2	18.8	56.0	51.7	41.93(+6.85/−3.22)	**Not Required**
Qwen3-32b	41.7	**21.1**	**58.6**	51.8	**43.30(+8.22/−1.85)**	
Qwen3-235b-a22b	**42.3**	20.7	57.3	52.4	43.18(+8.10/−1.97)	
Deepseek-v3	41.2	19.5	54.7	52.5	41.98(+6.90/−3.17)	

4.3 Verification of Domain Discriminating

To assess the effectiveness of our proposed methods in domain discriminating, we report three key metrics across four target domains: accuracy (Acc), fallback rate (Fbk), and error rate (Err). Table 5 presents the evaluation results for both the LLM as Router and LLM as Ranker strategies.

Router vs. Ranker. Results show that LLM as Router strongly depends on LLM capacity: small models like Qwen3-8b always go fallback (22.05% Acc, 73.68% Fbk), while larger models (e.g., Deepseek-v3) achieve competitive accuracy (72.40%) and low error rate (2.52%). By contrast, Ranker strategy provides rich context of multiple candidates to LLMs, notably benefiting smaller models (e.g., Qwen3-8b accuracy improves to 50.63%) while keeping error rates low.

These results confirm that domain inference signals from LLMs—especially when combined with fallback can reliably substitute for explicit domain labels, supporting plug-and-play adaptation to unknown domains.

Table 5. Domain discriminating scores in LLM as Router and LLM as Ranker strategies. Accuracy (Acc), Fallback rate (Fbk), and Error rate (Err) across four domains and overall average.

Model	IT			koran			law			medical			Average		
	Acc	Fbk	Err	Acc	Fbk	Err	Acc	Fbk	Err	Acc	Fbk	Err	Acc	Fbk	Err
LLM as Router															
Qwen3-8b	4.6	85.6	9.8	3.3	96.6	0.1	5.8	87.0	7.2	74.5	25.5	0.0	22.05	73.68	4.27
Qwen3-32b	87.2	11.6	1.2	70.3	21.2	8.5	67.1	12.1	20.8	80.2	8.2	11.6	76.20	13.27	10.53
Qwen3-235b-a22b	79.0	20.0	1.0	67.2	28.8	4.0	44.9	42.7	12.4	83.4	13.8	2.8	68.63	26.33	5.04
Deepseek-V3	54.1	44.9	1.0	80.7	18.4	0.9	73.8	20.2	6.0	81.0	16.8	2.2	72.40	25.08	2.52
LLM as Ranker															
Qwen3-8b	26.2	62.4	11.4	56.3	33.3	10.4	58.4	36.5	5.1	61.6	29.1	9.3	50.63	40.32	9.05
Qwen3-32b	29.9	61.3	8.8	81.2	16.9	1.9	68.5	27.8	3.7	55.0	35.8	9.2	58.65	35.45	5.90
Qwen3-235b-a22b	31.3	60.3	8.6	77.8	19.9	2.3	61.7	35.2	3.1	59.1	33.5	7.4	57.48	37.22	5.30
Deepseek-V3	24.7	71.0	4.3	49.2	50.0	0.8	43.0	55.5	1.5	58.2	36.8	5.0	43.78	53.33	2.89

4.4 Effectiveness of LCS Matching

To illustrate the necessity of LCS (Longest Common Subsequence) matching in enhancing the robustness of LLM as Ranker, we perform an ablation study, Table 6 presents the BLEU scores of various LLMs under the Ranker setting, with and without LCS matching. We observe consistent improvements across all models and domains when LCS matching is applied. For Deepseek-v3, it gains 16.7 BLEU in the IT domain and 6.2 BLEU in the medical domain. These gains are largely attributed to the removal of irrelevant text segments such as *"The best translation is..."* when the model neglects the instruction *"just output the result only"* and appends those texts.

These results indicate that LCS matching improves fidelity by filtering away explanatory or off-task content. It acts as a lightweight safeguard that guarantees translation quality without modifying model behavior.

Table 6. BLEU scores of LLM as Ranker strategy with and without LCS matching.

LLM		IT	koran	law	medical
Qwen3-8b	wo LCS	36.5	17.8	56.5	39.8
	with LCS	41.2	18.8	56.0	51.7
Qwen3-32b	wo LCS	36.5	17.8	56.5	39.8
	with LCS	41.7	21.1	58.6	51.8
Qwen3-235b-a22b	wo LCS	41.7	20.9	57.5	52.2
	with LCS	42.3	20.7	57.3	52.4
Deepseek-V3	wo LCS	24.5	15.6	48.5	46.3
	with LCS	41.2	19.5	54.7	52.5

4.5 Out-of-Domain Evaluation

Table 7. Out-of-domain translation performance on the IWSLT17 German-English test set(TED talks domain).

Model	BLEU
NMT	23.9
KNN-MT(IT)	14.1
KNN-MT(Koran)	6.5
KNN-MT(Law)	11.8
KNN-MT(Medical)	10.2
LLM as Router(Deepseek-v3)	21.6
LLM as Ranker(Qwen3-32b)	24.1

To evaluate the robustness of our method in out-of-domain scenarios, we tested on the TED talks transcripts from IWSLT17 dataset [42], which is not covered by any of the four KNN-MT experts. As shown in Table 7, KNN-MT expert models on mismatched domains yield significantly lower BLEU scores. In contrast, our method maintains competitive performance, LLM as Ranker even surpasses the original NMT model by effectively aggregating outputs from multiple expert models, indicating strong generalization.

5 Discussion

5.1 Generalizability to Other Expert Models

Our choice of KNN-MT as domain experts is motivated by its strong performance within specific domains and sharp degradation when applied to out-of-domain inputs. This makes it an ideal candidate for testing our methods. However, our proposed LLM-assisted framework is model-agnostic: it treats expert models as black boxes and makes no assumption about their internal structure. Therefore, it can be readily extended to incorporate other types of expert translation systems, including fine-tuned NMT models, adapter-based variants, or even commercial translation APIs specialized for different domains.

5.2 Risk of Over-Alignment on Safety

Public deployed LLMs are typically aligned with safety constraints and may refuse to respond when inputs violate safety policies. In our experiments, a few sentences triggered such safeguards, and the LLM declined to follow translation instructions. This behavior could limit the applicability of LLM-based methods in domains like military, cybersecurity, or hazardous materials. In this case, the system should fallback to using the general NMT model.

5.3 MoE in Multi-domain NMT

Mixture-of-Experts (MoE) architectures have shown great success in multilingual translation (e.g., NLLB-200 [1]). Multilingual models benefit from knowledge sharing, where language-specific experts can remain relatively independent due to the disjoint of nature languages. However, domains often exhibit more subtle and overlapping distinctions. Notably, the large MoE-based LLMs used in our experiments, Qwen3-235b-a22b and Deepseek-v3, do not perform well when directly used for domain-specified translation, suggesting that effective model-level multi-domain adaption remains an open problem.

6 Conclusion

We propose a simple yet effective method to improve domain adaptability in NMT without relying on domain labels. By leveraging LLMs through LLM as Router and LLM as Ranker strategies, our approach consistently outperforms LLM-only baselines and closely matches the performance of in-domain KNN-MT.

While promising, our work has limitations. We observed that larger LLMs (e.g., 235B, 671B) do not consistently outperform smaller ones (e.g., 32B) in the Ranker setting. Besides, in Ranker strategy, Qwen3-235b-a22b follows the instruction *just output the result only*, while other LLMs always excessively output. However, the reasons remain unclear. Future work could explore theoretical insights into LLM-scale behaviors. Additionally, integrating retrieval mechanisms may further improve the robustness and generalization of our method in real-world settings.

Acknowledgments. The research work descried in this paper has been supported by the National Key R&D Program of China (2020AAA0108001), and the National Nature Science Foundation of China (No. 62376019,62476023, 61976015, 61976016, 61876198 and 61370130). The authors would like to thank the anonymous reviewers for their valuable comments and suggestions to improve this paper.

Appendix

6.1 A Case Study on Youdao Translator

Youdao Translator is a well-known commercial machine translation service developed by NetEase, As a representative product of state-of-the-art neural machine translation (NMT) systems, it still requires domain labels from users. In case of example in Fig. 1, it produces these results[3]:

- General: Correct translation but colloquial.

[3] These results were tested on July 30, 2025.

通用场景 ⌄

Transformer 模型能够捕捉长距离的同指关系

以上翻译结果来自有道AI翻译标准模型· 通用场景

- Computer: Correct translation with proper terminology and professional linguistic style.

计算机 ⌄

Transformer模型可以捕获长距离共指

以上翻译结果来自有道神经网络翻译（YNMT）· 计算机

- Medical: Wrong translation on key terminologies.

医学 ⌄

变压器模型可以捕获远距离的相互参考

以上翻译结果来自有道神经网络翻译（YNMT）· 医学

- Finance and Economics: Wrong translation on key terminologies.

金融经济 ⌄

变压器模型可以捕获长距离的参考

以上翻译结果来自有道神经网络翻译（YNMT）· 金融经济

References

1. NLLB Team et al.: No language left behind: scaling human-centered machine translation (2022)
2. Goyal, N., et al.: The flores-101 evaluation benchmark for low-resource and multilingual machine translation. Trans. Assoc. Comput. Linguist. **10**, 522–538 (2022)

3. Vaswani, A., et al.: Attention is all you need. In: Advances in Neural Information Processing Systems, vol. 30 (2017)
4. Gu, S., Feng, Y.: Investigating catastrophic forgetting during continual training for neural machine translation. In: Proceedings of the 28th International Conference on Computational Linguistics, pp. 4315–4326 (2020)
5. van de Ven, G.M., Soures, N., Kudithipudi, D.: Continual learning and catastrophic forgetting (2024)
6. Khandelwal, U., et al.: Nearest neighbor machine translation. In: International Conference on Learning Representations (2021)
7. Moslem, Y., et al.: Adaptive machine translation with large language models. In: Proceedings of the 24th Annual Conference of the European Association for Machine Translation, pp. 227–237 (2023)
8. Agrawal, S., et al.: In-context examples selection for machine translation. In: Findings of the Association for Computational Linguistics: ACL 2023, pp. 8857–8873 (2023)
9. DeepSeek-AI, et al.: DeepSeek-V3 technical report (2025)
10. Aycock, S., Bawden, R.: Topic-guided example selection for domain adaptation in LLM-based machine translation. In: Proceedings of the 18th Conference of the European Chapter of the Association for Computational Linguistics: Student Research Workshop, pp. 175–195 (2024)
11. Zhang, B., Haddow, B., Birch, A.: Prompting large language model for machine translation: a case study (2023)
12. Bawden, R., Yvon, F.: Investigating the translation performance of a large multilingual language model: the case of BLOOM. In: Proceedings of the 24th Annual Conference of the European Association for Machine Translation, pp. 157–170 (2023)
13. Eschbach-Dymanus, J., et al.: Exploring the effectiveness of LLM domain adaptation for business IT machine translation. In: Proceedings of the 25th Annual Conference of the European Association for Machine Translation (Volume 1), pp. 610–622 (2024)
14. Zheng, J., et al.: Fine-tuning large language models for domain-specific machine translation (2024)
15. Yi, J., et al.: Benchmarking and defending against indirect prompt injection attacks on large language models. In: Proceedings of the 31st ACM SIGKDD Conference on Knowledge Discovery and Data Mining V.1, pp. 1809–1820 (2025)
16. Kompally, V.S.: A review of large language models in edge computing: applications, challenges, benefits, and deployment strategies. Int. J. Data Sci. Mach. Learn. **5**(01), 300–322 (2025)
17. Fang, Z., et al.: TEBNER: domain specific named entity recognition with type expanded boundary-aware network. In: Proceedings of the 2021 Conference on Empirical Methods in Natural Language Processing, pp. 198–207 (2021)
18. Oncevay, A., Smiley, C., Liu, X.: The impact of domain-specific terminology on machine translation for finance in European languages. In: Proceedings of the 2025 Conference of the Nations of the Americas Chapter of the Association for Computational Linguistics: Human Language Technologies (Volume 1: Long Papers), pp. 2758–2775 (2025)
19. Luong, M., Manning, C.: Stanford neural machine translation systems for spoken language domains. In: Proceedings of the 12th International Workshop on Spoken Language Translation: Evaluation Campaign, pp. 76–79 (2015)
20. Post, M., Vilar, " D.: Fast lexically constrained decoding with dynamic beam allocation for neural machine translation. In: Proceedings of the 2018 Conference of the North American Chapter of the Association for Computational Linguistics: Human Language Technologies, Volume 1 (Long Papers), pp. 1314–1324 (2018)

21. Song, K., et al.: Code-switching for enhancing NMT with pre-specified translation. In: Proceedings of the 2019 Conference of the North American Chapter of the Association for Computational Linguistics: Human Language Technologies, Volume 1 (Long and Short Papers), pp. 449–459 (2019)
22. Zhao, Y., et al.: Knowledge graph enhanced neural machine translation via multi-task learning on sub-entity granularity. In: Proceedings of the 28th International Conference on Computational Linguistics, pp. 4495–4505 (2020)
23. Britz, D., Le, Q., Pryzant, R.: Effective domain mixing for neural machine translation. In: Proceedings of the Second Conference on Machine Translation, pp. 118–126 (2017)
24. Koehn, P., Knowles, R.: Six challenges for neural machine translation. In: Proceedings of the First Workshop on Neural Machine Translation, pp. 28–39 (2017)
25. Wang, R., et al.: Sentence selection and weighting for neural machine translation domain adaptation. In: IEEE/ACM Transactions on Audio, Speech and Language Processing, vol. 26, no. 10, pp. 1727–1741 (2018)
26. Kobus, C., Crego, J., Senellart, J.: Domain control for neural machine translation (2017)
27. Gururangan, S., et al.: DEMix layers: disentangling domains for modular language modeling. In: Proceedings of the 2022 Conference of the North American Chapter of the Association for Computational Linguistics: Human Language Technologies, pp. 5557–5576 (2022)
28. Merx, R., et al.: Low-resource machine translation through retrieval-augmented LLM Prompting: a study on the Mambai language. In: Proceedings of the 2nd Workshop on Resources and Technologies for Indigenous, Endangered and Lesser-resourced Languages in Eurasia (EURALI) LREC-COLING 2024, pp. 1–11 (2024)
29. Tamura, T., et al.: Target language monolingual translation memory based NMT by cross-lingual retrieval of similar translations and reranking. In: Proceedings of Machine Translation Summit XIX, vol. 1: Research Track, pp. 313–323 (2023)
30. Cai, D., et al.: Neural machine translation with monolingual translation memory. In: Proceedings of the 59th Annual Meeting of the Association for Computational Linguistics and the 11th International Joint Conference on Natural Language Processing (Volume 1: Long Papers), pp. 7307–7318 (2021)
31. Aharoni, R., Goldberg, Y.: Unsupervised domain clusters in pretrained language models. In: Proceedings of the 58th Annual Meeting of the Association for Computational Linguistics, pp. 7747–7763 (2020)
32. Hu, T., et al.: Large language model for multi-domain translation: benchmarking and domain CoT fine-tuning. In: Findings of the Association for Computational Linguistics: EMNLP 2024, pp. 5726–5746 (2024)
33. Wang, J., et al.: Retrieval-augmented machine translation with unstructured knowledge (2024)
34. Yang, A., et al.: Qwen3 technical report (2025)
35. Zheng, X., et al.: Adaptive nearest neighbor machine translation. In: Proceedings of the 59th Annual Meeting of the Association for Computational Linguistics and the 11th International Joint Conference on Natural Language Processing (Volume 2: Short Papers), pp. 368–374 (2021)
36. Ji, Z., et al.: Survey of hallucination in natural language generation. ACM Comput. Surv. **55**(12) (2023)
37. Ng, N., et al.: Facebook FAIR′s WMT19 news translation task submission. In: Proceedings of the Fourth Conference on Machine Translation (Volume 2: Shared Task Papers, Day 1), pp. 314–319 (2019)
38. Post, M.: A call for clarity in reporting BLEU scores. In: Proceedings of the Third Conference on Machine Translation: Research Papers, pp. 186–191 (2018)
39. Rei, R., et al.: COMET: a neural framework for MT evaluation. In: Proceedings of the 2020 Conference on Empirical Methods in Natural Language Processing (EMNLP), pp. 2685–2702 (2020)

40. Zhu, W., et al.: kNN-BOX: a unified framework for nearest neighbor generation. In: Proceedings of the 18th Conference of the European Chapter of the Association for Computational Linguistics: System Demonstrations, pp. 10–17 (2024)
41. Johnson, J., Douze, M., Jégou, H.: Billion-scale similarity search with GPUs. IEEE Trans. Big Data **7**(3), 535–547 (2021)
42. Cettolo, M., et al.: Overview of the IWSLT 2017 evaluation campaign. In Proceedings of the 14th International Conference on Spoken Language Translation, pp. 2–14 (2017)
43. Dakwale, P., Monz, C.: Fine-tuning for neural machine translation with limited degradation across in- and out-of-domain data. In: Proceedings of Machine Translation Summit XVI: Research Track, pp. 156–169 (2017)
44. Wu, Q., et al.: Routing experts: learning to route dynamic experts in multi-modal large language models (2025)
45. Wang, C., Sennrich, R.: On exposure bias, hallucination and domain shift in neural machine translation. In: Proceedings of the 58th Annual Meeting of the Association for Computational Linguistics, pp. 3544–3552 (2020)

Author Index

J. Xu et al. (Eds.): CCMT 2025, CCIS 2906, p. 77, 2026.
https://doi.org/10.1007/978-981-92-0199-0

Zeitfracht Medien GmbH
Ferdinand-Jühlke-Straße 7
99095 Erfurt, Deutschland
produktsicherheit@kolibri360.de